CONVENIENT MYTHS

THE AXIAL AGE, DARK GREEN RELIGION, AND THE WORLD THAT NEVER WAS

IAIN PROVAN

BAYLOR UNIVERSITY PRESS

Cover Design by *the*BookDesigners

Cover Images ©Shutterstock/siloto, Rufous

Library of Congress Cataloging-in-Publication Data

Provan, Iain W. (Iain William), 1957-

  Convenient myths : the axial age, dark green religion, and the world that never was / Iain Provan.

  171 pages cm

  Includes bibliographical references and index.

  ISBN 978-1-60258-996-4 (hardback : alk. paper)

1. Religion and civilization. 2. Civilization, Ancient. 3. Myth--History. I. Title.

  BL55.P76 2013

  201'.693--dc23

                                        2013012318

For Lynette, Andrew, Kirsty, Duncan, and Catherine

CONTENTS

Preface   ix

Acknowledgments   xi

Introduction   1

1   The Turning Point of History   7
The Axial Age

2   Serious People, Bad Ideas   19
An Inquisition on the Axial Age

3   Procrustes and His Bed   29
Mutilating the Facts to Fit a Theory

4   Happy Hunting (and Gathering)   41
The Dark Green Golden Age

5   Hard Times in the Paleolithic   57
Constant Battles and Unequal Rights

6   Ecologically Noble Ancestors?   69
*Why Spiritual People Don't Necessarily Look
after Their Living Space*

7   You Can't Always Get What You Want   83
Desire (and Need) and the Past

8   The Past Reloaded   95
     A Brief History of Ancient Time

9   On Loving Your Dead Neighbor   107
     Violence, Knowledge, and History

10   On Truth and Consequences   121
     Why Myths about the Past Matter

Notes   129
Bibliography   145
Author Index   155
Subject Index   157

PREFACE

A word of explanation may be in order as to how a professional biblical scholar came to write a book that strays so far outside the area of his professional expertise. I first became interested in the two myths that lie at the heart of this book when I came across some of the writings of their propagators, and I noted just how poorly they were engaging with areas I do know something about, namely biblical literature, on the one hand, and ancient history, on the other. This led to further enquiries into the origins of the myths and into their reception history, including their critical reception. I was astonished just how influential they have been and continue to be, across a broad range of academic disciplines and (in some form or another) throughout popular culture. I was particularly intrigued to discover how immune they have apparently become to the many criticisms that have been advanced against them from various perspectives. This is mainly due (I think) to the fact that they are "big-picture" stories, while the criticisms have usually come from academics writing within narrow disciplinary boundaries, in journals and books that many people outside those disciplines do not read. It seemed to me, then, that there was a place for a book addressed to the general, literate reader, that might describe the myths, subject them to a critical gaze while making the specialist secondary literature accessible, and try to explain their popularity. All specialists do their work within the context of larger "stories," and we all need to engage with those stories from the perspective of our specialties if we are to ensure that the stories people believe (e.g., about the past) are actually true. This book is an attempt at such engagement, in part as a specialist and in part (inevitably) as an educated amateur.

Iain Provan
Vancouver, Canada, 2013

ACKNOWLEDGMENTS

This book and a closely related one—*Seriously Dangerous Religion: What the Old Testament Really Says and Why It Matters* (Baylor University Press, 2014)—were written over a period of several years, and I need to note my appreciation for both the institutions and the individual persons who offered me support and help as I was writing it.

On the institutional side, first of all, I need to thank my employers at Regent College for their support for the project by providing two periods of sabbatical leave in the winter semesters of 2009 and 2012. Thanks are also due, with respect to the second of these sabbaticals, to the University of Erfurt in Germany, and in particular to my host, Christoph Bultmann, and his wife Ursula, both of whom went out of their way to make my wife and me welcome. I must also thank most warmly the Alexander von Humboldt-Stiftung in Germany, who funded my stay in Erfurt, and the Lilly Foundation, whose Theological Research Grants Program covered our travel and other expenses.

On the personal side of things, I want to thank four research assistants at Regent College who completed an enormous amount of work on this project: Jen Gilbertson, Alex Breitkopf, Rachel Toombs, and Benjamin Petroelje. I also want to thank various people who advised me on the book proposal or read sections of the manuscript and made helpful comments: my wife Lynette, Dennis Danielson, John Stackhouse, Craig Gay, Phil Hanlon, Phil Long, and Scott and Monica Cousens. I am also most grateful to both Walter Brueggemann and Tremper Longman, who took the time to write supportive letters with respect to my application for the Lilly Foundation grant.

This book is dedicated to my immediate family—my wife and my four children. I am more proud of them all than I can say, and they have made me the person I am and (by extension) the author I am. Thank you all, wonderful people, for accompanying me on this journey.

Introduction

STAN FIELDS: What is the one most important thing our
society needs?
GRACIE HART: That would be harsher punishment
for parole violators, Stan.
(The crowd is silent)
GRACIE HART: And world peace!

—From the film *Miss Congeniality*

If we do not put a halt to it, civilization will continue to immiserate the vast majority of humans and to degrade the planet until it
(civilization, and probably the planet) collapses.

—Derrick Jensen, *Endgame*

We all believe at some level in world peace. That is why young women
in beauty pageants worldwide have so often asserted their own firm
commitment to it, as they have sought the judges' approval. It is such a
cliché that the 2000 film *Miss Congeniality* can exploit it for laughs—
among the many other aspects of beauty pageants that the film mocks.

Most of us also believe in saving the planet. I say "most of us," because
we must acknowledge the minority in different religious traditions who

1

cannot wait to see it blown to oblivion. Most of us, however, recognize that this is the only home we have right now, that some "inconvenient truths" have to be faced with respect to its sustainability, and that we have a moral obligation to deal with the problem as best we can.[1] We should not "degrade the planet."

These are both noble agenda items. It is possible, however, to become so driven by our visions of the future that we cannot see clearly what is right in front of our eyes, in the present. It is also possible to become so driven by these visions of the future that we cannot see clearly, either, what lies behind us, in the past. The past gets caught up in the future as we ask it to lend support to our *hopes* for the future, and we get confused about what is really there and how it is different from what we would only *like* to be there.

This is a book about the past—the world that was and the world that never was. It concerns two influential stories about the past told by well-meaning, intelligent, and idealistic people who believe in world peace and in saving the planet. I do want to stress *intelligent*. These are stories told by smart people, who are often writing at a very high level—professors and the like, writing peer-reviewed books and essays. Often "people in the street" will never have heard of these writers, even though they will certainly have been influenced by their ideas (whether they recognize it or not). These stories are persuasive. Unfortunately, they are untrue. They are myths—using *myth* in the modern, popular sense of "an unfounded or false notion."

The first of these stories I shall refer to as *the myth of the axial age*.[2] The idea of an axial age was first introduced to the world by the German existentialist philosopher Karl Jaspers in the period just after the Second World War. Jaspers had just lived through a period marked by barbarism, nationalism, and fanaticism. He was concerned, in the aftermath of the war, to identify something that modern human beings hold in common—something that might unify humanity and help us all to move forward together peaceably. He believed that he had discovered what was needed, not in any single religious or philosophical system, but in a specific historical experience: the axial age. Modern human beings stand, he proposed, on the far side of this crucial turning point in history (the period 800–200 BC). This is the period which produced the basic categories within which we modern human beings still carry on our thinking—the period that saw the emergence of world religions. The cultures that experienced this new beginning constantly return to it in order to renew themselves. They recognize as they do so what they hold in common, beyond all particular differences of faith. It is to this common past that we ourselves must *now* return, as we strive to make the unity of humankind concrete in the present. We must return to this axial age—the wellspring from which all faith once emerged, behind and beneath all specific religious and philosophical worldviews and their secularized, political forms. And, having gone back, we must move forward to build a new world order. We must birth a new axial age—an age of world peace.

Few of the readers of this book will have heard of Karl Jaspers. It is more likely that they will be familiar with some of the authors who have made axial age thinking more accessible to the general public—authors like the religious studies expert John Hick or the popular religious historian Karen Armstrong. They may not have encountered axial age thinking at a sophisticated level, then, but they will certainly have encountered it in the kind of unsophisticated statements that often appear in such books (e.g., statements about the ways in which all religions "are in essence really just the same," and about the present necessity of moving beyond absolutist ideologies to a more pluralist approach to truth). An increasing number of readers will also have encountered the myth of the axial age in educational curricula or privately by way of books emerging from the discipline of religious studies.

The second of the untrue stories at the heart of this book I shall refer to as *the myth of the dark green golden age*. This myth is in some respects older than the myth of the axial age. As we shall see later, some of its roots lie in previous notions of a past golden age that go back at least as far as the Renaissance. In its present form, the myth is specifically connected with what Bron Taylor in a recent book (2010) has called "dark green religion."[3] It is dark green both (he says) because it is very serious and because it is somewhat sinister. The storytellers in this case also believe in something like an axial age, but they do not look back to this age for inspiration. In the story told by dark green religionists, the axial age is one, not of enlightenment, but of repression. Axial age civilizations, they claim, destroyed prior societies based around natural and cosmological cycles. They broke the human connection with the earth. They also broke down human *community*, as *individual* religious identity developed. Axial age (world) religions, since they were not connected with particular places, inevitably reduced the importance of place, unless that "place" was in a spiritual afterlife. Much of what is wrong with contemporary human life results from this embrace of civilization. To recover ourselves, we must now *reject* civilization. We must get back behind the axial age, in order to recover a more authentic way of being. We must revisit the Paleolithic age and reconnect with our hunter-gatherer ancestors in the state of nature. Central to our recovery from civilization, in fact, will be the renewed embrace of preaxial spirituality. This is how we shall save the planet.

Again, not everyone will have heard of the key intellectuals who stand behind this myth of the dark green golden age, but many will have read accessible books that promote it, written by such notables as the ecologist David Suzuki and the anarcho-primitivist Derrick Jensen (who is quoted at the head of this introduction). They will very likely be familiar with some of the leading ideas, such as the notion that people in ancient hunter-gatherer societies lived much happier lives than we modern people do, or that they did a much better job of looking after the environment.

Both these stories have been told and retold in recent times by well-motivated people who want to make the world a better place. Both have proved to be remarkably influential, whether at sophisticated levels of politics and government (e.g., at the United Nations, as we shall see later) or at the more popular level. The popular appetite for the myths is well illustrated in the difficulty I faced, when writing this book, in getting access to the writings of people like Karen Armstrong and Derrick Jensen for any extended period of time, because of the demand for them in our local (including university) libraries. Certainly in the Pacific Northwest, in Canada (where I live), and in the United States, many people are drawn to these myths, and in recognition of the demand their proponents' books are well represented in our bookstores.

For my own part, I have enormous sympathy with the agendas of the writers in both camps. The problem I have is that I believe that each of the stories they tell in pursuit of these agendas is patently false, as I will show in chapters 1–6. They are *so* obviously false that it is hard to understand why so many smart, virtuous people have come to believe them. How is this possible? I consider this question in chapter 7, where I argue that there is a perennial danger in human intellectual activity regarding the past—the danger that desire and need, more than evidence, will drive our historical reconstructions. Both of the myths in question have important roles to play in many people's ideas about the present and their visions of the future. They need these prior ages in order to ground the message they want to proclaim about what we should believe and do now. They want these ages to exist. Desire and need have trumped sober judgment. The authors of the materials with which I engage in this book may well want *others* to embrace inconvenient truths; in the course of pressing these truths upon us, however, they *themselves* have unfortunately been seduced by convenient myths.

Why does this matter? First of all, we have a responsibility to tell the truth about the past, so far as we are able to do so. We have a responsibility not to do violence to it, just as we have a responsibility not to do violence in the present. Chapters 8 and 9 of the book are best taken, then, as my small attempt to help redress some wrongs that have been done to the past—to heal some wounds that have been inflicted by violent words. My focus is both general and specific. In chapter 8 I offer the reader an outline (and it is only that) of an accurate, overall account of the real ancient human past. In this presentation, the axial age naturally plays no part—neither as utopia nor as dystopia—and no golden age precedes it. The real past is rehabilitated as the fog of myth is dispelled. In chapter 9 I continue this theme in a more particular way. Mythmaking does not just distort the past in general. It also distorts the past in its particulars. Both the myths in question have certainly done this, profoundly misrepresenting various individual ancient religions and philosophies in pursuit of their fictions. I take as a case study in chapter 9 the area of my own expertise, which is the Old Testament biblical tradition, and I try to put on display the depth of misrepresentation and misunderstanding of this tradition that is evident among the proponents of both myths.

Second, what we believe about the past *is* inevitably bound up with our understanding of the present and our vision for the future. Our understanding of the past profoundly influences our decisions about the present and the future—just as our understanding of the present helps to shape our view of the past. This makes false notions of the past not just regrettable but dangerous. As Bobbi Low puts it (and I shall use this quotation again later), "Romantic misconceptions [about the past] might not matter, except that the conventional wisdoms arising from them generate normative prescriptions."[4] In chapter 10 I briefly illustrate the damage that can, in fact, be done in the present and as we move forward, when we embrace myths about the past rather than the truth. I show how the notion of the noble savage has proved detrimental to the human rights of native populations in Latin America, and how notions of an ancient "pristine wilderness" have proved to be an obstacle to sensible wilderness care in the United States.

In the end we contribute neither to world peace nor to saving the planet by romanticizing the past. We must ensure that our story about the past is not at odds with the evidence, precisely so that we do not end up harming the very people—the very planet—that we are so intent, in our well-meaning way, on trying to save.

The Turning Point of History
The Axial Age

> . . . the most crucial turning point in history; it was then that
> man as he is today was born . . . the "axial age."

> —Karl Jaspers, "The Axial Age of Human History"

> I believe that we are in a Second Axial Period. We are caught up
> in a transformation of consciousness that is as momentous as
> that of the First Axial Period and that will have comparable far-
> reaching effects on religion and spirituality.

> —Ewert Cousins, "Spirituality in Today's World"

The myth of the axial age has been widely embraced throughout the
world in the course of the last several decades, whether consciously and
at first hand or more unconsciously and at a distance, as its core message has seeped out into both serious and popular culture. It originated
from the mind of the German existentialist philosopher Karl Jaspers,
although Jaspers built on various precursors.[1]

THE STORYTELLER
KARL JASPERS (1948–1953)

In an essay published in 1948, Jaspers looks back upon the record of history telling in the West up until that point and suggests that it has hitherto been grounded to an unacceptable extent in a specifically Christian account of the world.[2] The turning point or "axis" of human history has been wrongly identified as the entrance of Jesus Christ into the world. This faith-based approach to the past must now be rejected. "If there does exist such a thing as an axis, or turning point, in history," Jaspers affirms,

> it must be based on observable or recorded fact; and it must be valid for all men, including Christians. Such an axis would be that point in history where man first discovered the notion of himself that he has realized since, the point in time where there occurred that shaping of man's being which has produced the most important results. And the existence of this turning point would have to be, if not absolutely demonstrable, at least convincing on an empirical basis for Europeans, for Asiatics, and for all men, without the need to appeal to the criterion of a definite religious doctrine. Only thus could it provide a common frame of historical self-understanding.

It is, in fact, in the period 800–200 BCE, he continues, that we find "the most crucial turning point in history; it was then that man as he is today was born."[3] He calls this period, therefore, the axial age.

This was the age in China of both Confucius and Laozi (the founder of Daoism). In India it was the age of the Upanishads and Buddha; in Iran, Zoroaster; in Palestine, the Hebrew prophets; and in Greece, Homer, Parmenides, Heraclitus, Plato, Thucydides, and Archimedes. It was an era, therefore, during which what are still the fundamental categories that we use in our modern thinking were developed. It was the era of the beginnings of the world religions by whose teachings we have lived until the present time—an age in which "a step was made towards the universal." The age of myth was over. Rationality and practical experience now battled against myth, and religion became informed by ethics. The human condition was transformed in a way that may be described as a spiritualization. There are great differences among the various faiths that arise out of the axial age, Jaspers acknowledges, but "they all alike come to serve as instruments by which man transcends himself, by which he becomes aware of his own being within the whole of Being, and by which he enters upon pathways that he must travel as an individual. . . . What took place in this axial age was the discovery of what was later to be called reason and personality." In this transcending of the self, humanity leapt forward, although the potentialities released at this time were never fully realized, since the masses could not follow the enlightened individuals in whom the transformation was occurring. It is to this new beginning, however, that humanity ever returns, in China, India, and the West, in its renaissances and new spiritual surges, recollecting and retrieving the possibilities of the axial age. Indeed, "when the three worlds that experienced the axial age meet with one another, a profound understanding is possible. They recognize when they meet that their concerns are the same."[4] There is no truth common to all three that can be put into an objective statement; nevertheless, they share authentic and unconditional truth. At the same time, people living outside these three worlds have either remained outside the stream of history as primitive peoples, or they have been drawn into it by coming into contact with one of the three and have been assimilated.

What does this mean? Jaspers argues:

> Really to see the axial age, to gain it as a foundation for our universal view of history, means: to gain something that is common to all mankind above and beyond all differences of faith. It is one thing to see the unity of history only from the background of one's own faith; it is quite another to conceive the unity of history in communication with every other human background, combining one's own consciousness with that which is foreign to one. In this sense, it may be said of the centuries between 800 and 200 BCE that they constitute the empirically ascertainable axis of history for *all* men.[5]

The reality of the axial age, then, "summons [us] to boundless communication," prompting us to overcome our narrowness and to oppose the claim that any one faith exclusively possesses the truth. It calls us to arms against fanaticism, pride, and self-deception—against the will to power that dominates Western thought in particular. We are summoned to acknowledge the empirical truth, that "God has revealed himself historically in many ways and opened up many paths to himself. It is as if God, speaking the language of universal history, were warning us against exclusive claims." This discovery must then affect our understanding of our contemporary situation, in which we must ask ourselves how the unity of the human race can become a concrete reality for each of us, whatever our own tradition may be.[6]

In the book that arose out of this same research and thinking, published in the following year (1949) and subsequently appearing in English translation in 1953, Jaspers lays out his own vision of the future, in the light of the past: "Even the great spiritual powers handed down to us no longer support life . . . we must return to a deeper origin, to a fountainhead from which all faith once welled forth in its particular historical shapes, to this wellspring which can flow at any time man is ready for it. . . . [T]rust in the origin of all things must lay the foundations." He goes on to envisage a new religious order—a new axial age: "In coming centuries men will perhaps arise who, sustained by the sight of the origin of the Axial Period, will proclaim truths replete with the knowledge and experience of our era that will really be believed and lived," taking into account that "the truth of faith lies in the multiplicity of its historical manifestations, in the self-encountering of this multiplicity through ever deeper communication." In the meantime, he tells us, "Every individual must know where he stands and for what he will work. It is as though everyone were charged by the Deity to work and live for boundless openness, authentic reason, truth and love and fidelity, without the recourse to force that is typical of the States and Churches in which we have to live and whose insufficiency we should like to oppose."[7]

THE LISTENERS (1980–2005)

The idea that an axial age could be identified in this way, as a matter of observable or recorded fact in the past—that the centuries between 800 and 200 BCE constitute the empirically ascertainable axis of history for all people—did not apparently take hold of the general imagination immediately.[8] Certainly from at least the 1980s onward, however, we begin to see the axial age mentioned in print with more and more frequency simply as a datum of the past. In some of this writing, we find reference also to a second axial age in our present or future.

Ewert Cousins

One of the most significant channels through which Jaspers' thinking was communicated to others appears to have been Ewert Cousins, an early pioneer in interreligious dialogue and an influential figure in his time. He was the moving spirit behind the Classics of Western Spirituality series of classical works from the Christian, Jewish, and Muslim traditions and the general editor of the series World Spirituality: An Encyclopedic History of the Religious Quest. In 1975 he helped to coordinate the "Spiritual Summit Conference" at the United Nations (the first interfaith conference held there), and in 1998 he cofounded the World Commission on Global Consciousness and Spirituality, one of whose objectives is to "find deeper common ground between differing worldviews."[9] He also helped with the planning and design of the three Parliaments of the World's Religions held in Chicago (1993), Cape Town (1999) and Barcelona (2004). Writing in 1987, Cousins reviewed the then-recent "awakening of spirituality" in the West as a result of influence from the East, noting both its religious and its secular forms (e.g., the development of psychotherapy).[10] He offers his own theory about the emergence of what he thinks of as a "global spirituality." In order to understand this phenomenon, he asserts, we must view it from a long-range historical perspective. We must begin with the axial age identified by Jaspers—a period when a consciousness developed that was vastly different from that of preceding archaic, primitive, or tribal peoples. This new consciousness, marked above all by a sense of individual identity, has now become the dominant form of consciousness in the world: "By far the majority of the world's population possesses the form of consciousness that took shape in the Axial Period."[11] The axial age

> released a burst of spiritual energy whose influences are being felt even to this day. . . . The new individual consciousness could look within and find the divine in the depths of the soul. It could follow the light of its own conscience even against the opinions of the many. It could strike out alone on a journey leading to enlightenment or union with the divine. These journeys tended to take the form of an ascent: from the material to the spiritual to the divine. With extraordinary enthusiasm, the Axial spiritual seeker freed himself from the constraints of

matter and climbed the lofty mountain of the spirit towards its divine summit.[12]

Cousins then offers the opinion that we find ourselves now in a second axial age. We are presently caught up in a second transformation of consciousness that is just as momentous as the first. However, whereas the first axial age produced *individual* consciousness, the second is producing *global* consciousness. This is true in two senses. First, people are "beginning to feel their primary relatedness not to their nation or culture, but to the human community as a whole," and second, we are also newly aware of our responsibility toward the earth. The "second Axial spirituality" that must accompany this transformation of consciousness must likewise be global, in both senses.[13] It must expand its horizons, through empathetic interreligious dialogue, "to include the spiritualities of the entire human community"; and it must "recover its rootedness in the earth, in matter, in biology," recovering dimensions of spirituality lost in the transition into the first axial consciousness.[14] "The future of the human race [itself]," Cousins claims, "will largely depend on the success of the world's religions to develop an adequate spirituality of the Second Axial Period. . . . There is reason to think that the creative development of global spirituality, through interreligious dialogue, is the distinctive spiritual journey of our time."[15]

Subsequent Writers

By the 1990s we find the axial age routinely alluded to as an important reference point for various reconstructions of the past, as well as for policies in the present and imaginings of (or advocacy with respect to) the future. Writing a postscript in 1994 to a volume of essays on Roman Catholic approaches to ecology, Wayne Teasdale outlines various elements of a solution to our planet's ongoing environmental troubles under the heading "Toward a Second Axial Age." He mentions the necessity of interfaith relations and of the Catholic Church's commitment to interreligious dialogue. He also advocates for the Parliament of the World's Religions, predicting (and referencing Jaspers in doing so) that "the 1993 Parliament . . . will be seen in time as an axial event-process, because it has inaugurated deep and far-reaching changes in human consciousness." He further commends nonviolence as a primary value as well as the deployment of the spiritual resources found in nature-mysticism and contemplation, on the way to a global spirituality. The great task of the next millennium, he asserts, "is the evolution of a universal civilization predicated on ecological awareness and responsibility, a global society and culture animated by compassion, kindness, love, and humanity, living in sustainable and harmonious relationship with the earth. . . . All of our utopian dreams, recorded in many of our myths, will be realized when this new spiritual society dawns."[16]

Writing in a rather different context, Carlton Tucker describes his use of Jaspers' model of the axial age (albeit that he describes it as lasting from around 600 BCE to 600 CE) in teaching history, since it is a "unifying period of World history and World religions" and enables "a better understanding of today's contemporary, 'New Age' world . . . [which represents] another breakthrough moment because of the meeting of World religions on such a vast scale."[17] Yves Lambert also builds on Jaspers in his characterization of modernity as a new axial age, out of which new forms of consciousness are evolving and will continue to evolve.[18]

The idea of an historical axial age continues to exert its influence in the 2000s and down to our present moment; and again, in some of the literature, it is explicitly linked to a *new* axial age. Michael Barnes makes significant use of the first axial age in his treatment of intellectual history, devoting a whole chapter to this age and to the classical style of thought.[19] Elise Boulding looks forward to a new axial age in the coming millennium.[20] Gananath Obeyesekere presupposes the first axial age when writing about the way in which prevailing secular social morality was redefined as religious morality in different religious environments in that historical period.[21] Roger Gillette adopts the position that we are currently developing a new global worldview so radically different from previous ones as to mark the emergence of a new axial age. This calls for a new religion that is markedly different from any of the current world religious traditions.[22] Writing in the year following Gillette's essay, William Herbrechtsmeier makes use of the axial age idea in an essay focusing on aspects of religion as functions of social and political concerns.[23]

One of the best-known modern writers on religion is John Hick, whose embrace of the same axial age concept is well illustrated in his *Interpretation of Religion*.[24] In this book Hick freely employs the language of "pre-axial," with respect to archaic forms of religion like the religions of the Stone Age or of ancient Egypt, Greece and Rome, India,

and China. He uses the language of "axial" (or "post-axial") with respect
to religions of salvation or liberation that find their roots "in what Karl
Jaspers has identified as the *Achsenzeit* [Axial Age]"[25]—what we now
know as the great world faiths. For Hick, it is indeed a "widely accepted
large-scale interpretive concept" that there is "a distinction between
pre-axial religion, centrally (but not solely) concerned with the pres-
ervation of cosmic and social order, and post-axial religion, centrally
(but not solely) concerned with the quest for salvation or liberation."[26]
The level of acceptance of at least an *historical* axial age is further illustrated in Steven Smith's 2005 philosophical study of appeal (that which
commands our attention in the world) and attitude (the quality of the
attention we pay to it). Smith grounds two of his chapters in the axial
age: "Appeal in the Axial Age" (chapter 2) and "Attitude in the Axial
Age" (chapter 6).[27] Mario Liverani's history of Israel devotes a chapter
to the axial age,[28] and an essay by biblical scholar William Morrow on
early Jewish penitential prayers depends significantly on the idea.[29]

THE POPULARIZER
KAREN ARMSTRONG (2005–2006)

As our brief and selective account above reveals, the concept of an axial
age was already well accepted in various quarters by the mid-2000s. It
had made a significant impact across different disciplines and in both
the academic and the popular world. John Hick counts, I think, as an
early popularizer. Without question, however, the idea also received
fresh exposure as a result of the popular books published in the middle
of the decade by Karen Armstrong, a well-known British author and
media personality who was first noted as a result of her earlier volume,
A History of God.[30]

A Short History of Myth

In 2005 Armstrong published *A Short History of Myth*, a brief and
highly readable book that sought to answer these questions: What are
myths? How have they evolved? And why do we still so desperately
need them? By way of answering these questions, Armstrong tells a
story about human religious development, beginning in the Paleolithic
period (20,000–8000 BCE). She understands religious sentiment at
this time as arising from such realities as the impressiveness of the sky,
the dangers of the hunt, a sense of solidarity with the animals, and

unconscious male resentment of the female. Later, with the development of agriculture in the Neolithic period (8000–4000 BCE), there was "a great spiritual awakening that gave people an entirely new understanding of themselves and their world." Farming, like hunting before it, became sacramental; the sacred was encountered in the earth and its agricultural products. The earth became Mother Goddess; the gods and creatures were regarded as one reality; sex and agriculture became two sides of the same coin. Next came the early civilizations (4000–800 BCE), where a sense that people were the masters of their own destiny developed, and the gods became more remote. It was this spiritual vacuum that in due course produced a second great transformation in the axial age (800–200 BCE), which "marks the beginning of religion as we know it."[31] All the axial movements that arose in this period had essential ingredients in common:

> They were acutely conscious of the suffering that seemed an inescapable part of the human condition, and all stressed the need for a more spiritualized religion that was not so heavily dependent upon external rituals and practice. They had a new concern about the individual conscience and morality. . . . All the sages recoiled from the violence of their time, and preached an ethic of compassion and justice. They taught their disciples to look within themselves for truth and not to rely on the teachings of priests and other religious experts. Nothing should be taken on trust, everything should be questioned, and old values . . . must be subjected to critical scrutiny.[32]

The remainder of the book is relatively brief, taking us in forty-six pages through the postaxial period (up to 1500 CE) and then the great Western transformation (from 1500 until 2000 CE). The closing pages provide us with Armstrong's understanding of the present and the vision of the future that is connected with her understanding of the past. If we are to save our planet, she tells us, we need myths that among other things will teach us about the importance of compassion and help us "venerate the earth as sacred once again."[33] Here Jaspers' axial age is integrated, as a key structural element, into a well-told story about past, present, and future that is accessible to a relatively average reader.

The Great Transformation

Armstrong followed up this book with another, much longer one in 2006, entitled *The Great Transformation: The Beginning of our Religious Traditions*. Its opening pages explicitly set the present context in which her examination of the past will be carried out: "Perhaps every generation believes that it has reached a turning point of history, but our problems seem particularly intractable and our future increasingly uncertain. Many of our difficulties mask a deeper spiritual crisis. . . . Religion, which is supposed to help us cultivate [a sense of the sacred inviolability of each human person], often seems to reflect the violence and desperation of our times." In the midst of this analysis she repeats some of the language of the closing pages of her 2005 book on myth, and she adds to it: "Unless there is some kind of spiritual revolution that can keep abreast of our technological genius, it is unlikely that we will save our planet. A purely rational education will not suffice." The importance of Jaspers' work to Armstrong then becomes particularly clear: "In our current predicament, I believe that we can find inspiration in the period that . . . Karl Jaspers called the Axial Age." This was an age, Armstrong alleges, in which the important matter was not what a person's beliefs were but how that person acted. Religion was about action. It *was* compassion; it *was* (from the perspective of the sages of the axial age) "respect for the sacred rights of all beings." It is this axial ethos that we must now recover, rejecting parochial or exclusive visions and joining the spiritual quest of the whole human race, centered on the compassionate ethic about which all the axial sages speak. Armstrong returns to this same theme in summary fashion at the end of the book: "At their core the Axial faiths share an ideal of sympathy, respect, and universal concern. . . . Regardless of their theological 'beliefs'—which, as we have seen, did not much concern the sages—they all concluded that if people made a disciplined effort to reeducate themselves, they would experience an enhancement of their humanity . . . an alternative state of consciousness." The axial age thinkers needed to come up with a new vision of existence because, socially and psychologically, humanity had taken a great leap forward. So, too, do we.[34]

THE LISTENERS (2006–2012)

The years since 2006 have by no means diminished the flow of books, essays, and Internet postings that depend on the Jaspers thesis—and indeed often specifically on the Armstrong popularization of this thesis.[35] I mention here just six.

First, Hans Joas characterizes Europe as an axial age culture, although rather curiously (in view of everything I have written above) he asserts that this term "has not yet become a part of everyday language."[36] Robert Engelman, second, spends an entire chapter on the axial age in the course of his study of population growth, women's lives, and the interaction of both with nature.[37] Third, we may note Hoda Mahmoudi's essay on modernity from the perspective of the Baha'i faith. As it traverses history, religion (she claims) "draws from the timeless universal spiritual teachings revealed in all the major world religions. However, each successive religious revelation unfurls new knowledge and understanding that conform to the changes and challenges of its particular age, causing the steady edification of human consciousness." For Mahmoudi, Jesus, Mohammed, and the rest are simply the spiritual teachers of history, "the animating forces in the rise of civilizations through which consciousness has flowered."[38] A case in point where spiritual educators have done this is the axial age—one of only a number of collapses in the established order, historically, that have led on to a major spiritual revival. Today we are dealing with a new collapse at a global level, and we need to move toward a new unity:

> As in the former civilizations of the Axial Age, or the society that blossomed during the Renaissance, the Enlightenment, and now in the modern world, the waters of the river of divine revelation continue to channel the whole of humanity toward "an ever-advancing civilization" . . . destined to progressively and over time evolve into a planetary commonwealth.[39]

Fourth, in 2009 biblical scholar Baruch Halpern published a volume of essays from his preceding twenty-seven years of writing. The preface asserts that they contribute to "the study of historiography in ancient Israel (and beyond) during Karl Jaspers' Axial Age."[40] Fifth, the axial age finds a prominent place in Mark Muesse's 2011 book, *The Hindu Traditions*, where it is embraced as the context within which "the characteristic features of what we may call the classical era [of Hinduism] came into view."[41] And finally, the axial age is a key interpretive concept in Robert Bellah's narrative concerning the history of religion in the centuries before Christ in his book (also published in 2011), *Religion in Human Evolution: From the Paleolithic to the Axial Age.*[42]

AN APPRECIATION . . . AND A QUESTION

The story of the axial age is evidently a popular story, in more than one sense of the word. Clearly, many people find this story to be persuasive, to some degree or another, and for many it contributes significantly to their sense of who they are, where they should be heading, and what they should do next. This is true whether or not they accept the idea that we are living in a second axial age, although it is particularly true for those who do.

It is, of course, entirely commendable that so many people, particularly in this second group, are urging us all toward what is virtuous and away from what is not. It is certainly no part of my purpose in this book to commend what Karl Jaspers refers to as fanaticism, human pride, or self-deception through the will to power. I am certainly not about to oppose what he refers to as authentic reason, truth, love, and fidelity. I am as much an advocate as Karen Armstrong of a compassionate ethic, and I seek to live my life in conformity with such an ethic. As I stated in my introduction, the myths I discuss in this book have been created by well-meaning people who want to make the world a better place— people who believe that we are in trouble just now, and that we face a huge challenge in carving out a better future. I stand by that statement, and I affirm the good in much of what those who recount the axial age story have to say. Genuine dialogue among all the peoples of the earth is certainly something to be advanced by all possible means, and care for the planet upon which we live is not only our duty but has now become a necessity if it (and we) are to survive at all.

Yet with all that said, my questions remain: Was there ever really an axial age, historically? Is it really true? Is it a matter of "observable or recorded fact . . . convincing on an empirical basis"?[43]

SERIOUS PEOPLE, BAD IDEAS
An Inquisition on the Axial Age

The Confucian reworking of much older Chinese traditions
differs in fundamental ways from the Jewish counter-model to
Egyptian "political theology," even though the pre-axial past is
the context in which the new paradigm emerges. The case of
Greece is different again; and of India, different once more.

—Johann Arnason, "The Axial Age and Its Interpreters"

A Chinese personal existence under the cosmic *tao*, or an Indian
personal existence in acosmistic illumination, is not an Israelite
or Christian existence under God.

—Eric Voegelin, *Order and History*

As a way into the discussion that follows, we may begin with a significant, fairly recent critique of Karl Jaspers' thought by Johann Arnason.[1] Ironically, in view of Jaspers' appeal to observable or recorded fact,
Arnason criticizes Jaspers *precisely* for a lack of careful attention to
empirical historical data in his theorizing. In fact, he understands Jaspers' various claims, "including some of his most aberrantly unhistori-
cal statements[,] . . . as attempts to settle, bypass or neutralize unstated
problems to which we must return."[2]

JOHANN ARNASON ON KARL JASPERS

One of the most fundamental problems, claims Arnason, is the very sharp distinction that Jaspers makes between preaxial, "unawakened" cultures and their successors. We simply do not know enough about all the preaxial cultures to be able to generalize about them in this way, and what we do know tells against any notion of uniformity. The circumstances under which individual cultures moved from a preaxial to an axial condition likewise varied. When Jaspers describes the common denominator of the axial breakthroughs in terms of a change of consciousness in which "man becomes conscious of Being as a whole, of himself and his limitations" and "experiences absoluteness in the depths of selfhood and in the lucidity of transcendence,"[3] he is doing nothing less (says Arnason) than imposing an anachronistic model on history arising from his own existentialist philosophical commitments.

One important aspect of Jaspers' lack of attention to historical detail lies in his description of the social context of the alleged spiritual breakthrough in the axial age. Jaspers envisages small states and cities engaging in fruitful economic competition leading to fundamental change. The problem here is that we do not actually find invariant patterns of state formation to which the various axial transformations can be linked. China and Greece are very different from each other, for example. With respect to India, we can make "some kind of connection between state formation in the eastern Ganges plain and the rise of Buddhism, but it is much less obvious what the Upanishads might have had to do with that kind of background."[4] The situation in Israel is quite different again—one small state dominated by various empires.[5]

A similar problem arises with respect to Jaspers' understanding of the transition from the axial to the postaxial age. For Jaspers "the Axial Age ended everywhere in unequivocal decline" in conjunction with imperial resurgence (e.g., in the Hellenistic and Roman Empires). There was a return to the preaxial phase of history (although the postaxial empires depended on axial sources at an ideological level). As Arnason argues, however, the actual historical reality is much more complex. There is no uniform pattern to the relationships of imperial formations with "axial legacies." For example, "an imperial background . . . seems to have been essential to the legacy which the most lastingly influential current of axial thought in China wanted to preserve and refine." Empire remained crucial. In India, the Mauryan Empire "was perhaps . . . at one point more receptive to axial innovations than any other contemporary state."[6] Empire and axial innovations were not at odds with each other.

Finally, Arnason takes issue with Jaspers' claim that between the three axial regions "*a profound mutual comprehension was possible* from the moment they met. . . . [T]hey recognized that they were concerned with the same problems."[7] To this Arnason responds as follows: "I do not think that the rest of the book does much to back up this astonishing statement, and it would be all too easy to marshal evidence against it from modern history."[8] There *is* a globalizing potential in the various axial ideas as they come to expression within each civilization, Arnason agrees, but the history of encounters between these civilizations is complicated and is never superseded by the condition that Jaspers describes as "boundless communication."

Shmuel Eisenstadt

Arnason follows up this devastating assessment of Jaspers' genuine objectivity with an account of a major, more recent attempt to develop a theory about the axial age that pays more serious attention to the historical record: the work of Shmuel Eisenstadt. (He also mentions but does not discuss the work of Eric Voegelin, to whom I shall return below.)[9] Throughout his work Eisenstadt argues that the common denominator in axial breakthroughs is "the emergence, conceptualization and institutionalization of a basic tension between the transcendental and mundane orders." The belief emerges that there is another dimension, a "higher transcendental moral or metaphysical order which is beyond any given this- or other-worldly reality,"[10] as (for example) in Greece, where the belief emerged that there was an impersonal world order beyond the gods. Such a belief is then translated into new institutions, projects, and practices. Eisenstadt does not regard this distinction between two orders of reality as an axial invention, but he does think that there is a radicalization of the distinction within axial civilizations. This radicalization has significant implications for the future of each civilization, as an order-transforming social dynamic comes to prevail over an order-maintaining one. The axial age lays the foundations for subsequent social transformations in general and modern social transformations in particular (especially those of a revolutionary nature).[11]

Arnason on Eisenstadt

Arnason acknowledges that Eisenstadt is "far more sensitive to the historical realities and experiences of early civilizations than Jaspers was," and in connection with this he applauds his general lack of reference to "universalistic orientations as a defining feature of axial civilizations." Yet, as the second epigraph to this chapter illustrates, he still believes that Eisenstadt's account fails to do justice to the *differences* among the axial civilizations, not least in the varied ways in which they relate to their pasts. For Arnason, Eisenstadt also fails to pay sufficient attention to the very different political environments out of which the axial age civilizations emerged—environments that without question shaped the realities that *did* emerge. In China, for example, the unparalleled conquest of the civilizational center of the culture by a peripheral state may be cited as a possible reason why the axial transformation in China followed a different course from transformations elsewhere.[12]

Moreover, in reference to Eisenstadt's common denominator that axial cultures distinguished between the transcendental and the mundane, Arnason insists that we must take account of the fact that "the two levels of order relate to each other in different ways in the various axial traditions, and the meaning lent to their relationship depends on the overall logic of the respective worldview."[13] We must move beyond generalizations about the transcendental and the mundane to examine the individual cultures themselves and the precursors to which they relate. For example, where Eisenstadt claims (with respect to the axial age in general) that "the King-God, the embodiment of the cosmic and earthly order alike, disappeared, and a secular ruler, in principle accountable to some higher order, appeared,"[14] Arnason rightly notes that "this formulation appears to equate sacred kingship with its most emphatic form: the terms quoted above are clearly more applicable to Egypt than to Mesopotamia, and the question of accountability—as an innovation—would have to be posed in more nuanced terms."[15]

Arnason sums up his interaction with Eisenstadt by claiming that the latter's idea of an axial breakthrough is open to various critical questions, some of which are closely connected with the questions he (Arnason) raises about Jaspers' own work.[16] He thinks of Eisenstadt's work only as a guide to further exploration in the field, and he looks forward to a future in which there will be "a more balanced combination of theoretical and historical perspectives." It is interesting, however, that, in an unpublished paper delivered to the Central European University Department of History in January 2011, entitled "Re-historicizing the Axial Age," Arnason appears to have to come to regard Eisenstadt's influence on the discussion as positively unhelpful, particularly in its emphasis on the common denominator among axial cultures.[17] The search for a common denominator is premature, he suggests. We need more comparative analysis of the relevant cases and a better understanding of their interrelations. Arnason urges renewed attention, therefore, to the empirical data relating to the axial age.

Reflections

It is not clear to me that Arnason's criticism of Eisenstadt is entirely fair, at least in one respect: the extent of Eisenstadt's recognition of diversity among the so-called axial civilizations. In a book like *Fundamentalism, Sectarianism, and Revolution* (1999), for example, Eisenstadt does try to show what these civilizations had in common over time—not least that "there continually developed within them alternative, competing transcendental visions." He is also clear, though, about what differentiated them in terms of how far (or whether) they institutionalized these transcendental visions in their pristine forms, and about what part their views of divine revelation and reason played in this process. The various compromises reached on such matters differed from each other (he claims) as a result of the various "basic ontological conceptions of the nature of the chasm between the transcendental and the mundane spheres and of the ways of bridging this chasm . . . the conception of the political arena and its place in the implementation of the transcendental visions . . . [and] the extent of acceptance and possible legitimization of the utilitarian, egoistic dimensions of human nature."[18] He explores these differences among "otherworldly civilizations," like those dominated by Buddhism and Hinduism; "this-worldly civilizations" that have not been monotheistic, like Confucian China; and the monotheistic civilizations shaped by Judaism, Christianity, and Islam (which is included here even though its origins lie "beyond the Axial Age proper").[19] Historically, otherworldly civilizations have not viewed politics as the primary arena in which the transcendental vision should be realized. This-worldly nonmonotheistic civilizations, however, *have* viewed the political arena in such a way. Monotheistic civilizations have seen the reconstruction of the mundane world in the light of the transcendental as *one* of the required tasks.[20]

These various compromises have then been subject, in each civilization down through the ages, to very different responses by utopian sectarians—those whose lives have been captivated particularly intensely by the transcendental vision. In the otherworldly case, we find no "strong alternative conceptions of the social and, in particular, the political orders." The transcendental vision did not "touch down" in social and political reality. In the this-worldly nonmonotheistic case, intermittent utopian visions "did not lead to far-reaching institutional reconstruction of the political centers of the society," and their promoters "rarely challenged the basic premises of the regimes or of the political order." In the monotheistic case, however, we find "strong tendencies to the development of some visions of different political and, to some extent, social orders based on the reconstruction of the basic ontologies prevalent" in the respective civilizations.[21] The transcendental vision *did* "touch down" in social and political reality.

For the purposes of the argument I am developing here, however, I do not need to adjudicate between Eisenstadt and Arnason in terms of the latter's being *completely* fair to the former. Arnason's critique is damaging enough in its overall thrust, even if it can be challenged in part. Certainly enough has been said to this point to raise serious questions about the kind of large-scale theorizing about an axial age that is found in the work of Jaspers, in particular, and of Eisenstadt, to a lesser extent.

FURTHER CONTRIBUTIONS

It is not difficult to find other books and essays that likewise either explicitly or implicitly (and indeed sometimes accidentally), as a result of their analysis, cast doubt on the claim that there was an axial age.

Eric Voegelin

As mentioned above, Arnason cites Voegelin as attempting (along with Eisenstadt) to develop a more systematic theory about the axial age than Jaspers. This is, however, a somewhat strange way of putting things, for Voegelin is, in fact, stringent in his criticism of Jaspers' whole notion of an axial age. In volume 2 of *Order and History*, published in 1957, Voegelin agrees that there was in the ancient world what he calls a "leap of being" in various places, in which there emerged new truth about reality beyond the truth of ancient myth. This is not in the end *one* leap, however, but rather a *plurality* of leaps that "differ widely with regard to the radicalism of their break with the cosmological myth, as well as with regard to the comprehensiveness and penetration of their advance toward the truth about the order of being." These differences should not be underestimated (again, as the second epigraph to this chapter suggests). Voegelin is, in fact, critical of Jaspers (and Arnold Toynbee) because, while their respect for each society and its attempts to articulate truth is laudable, "this respect . . . must not degenerate into a tolerance which disregards the differences of rank, both in the search for truth and the achievement of insight."[22] He continues,

> The generous thesis of Jaspers, for instance, that in the axis-time were "created the fundamental categories in which we think to this day," will appear doubtful if we consider concretely that the Aristotelian *Analytica Posteriora*, the fundamental work on analytical thinking to this day, was created, not . . . in China or India, but in Hellas [Greece]; and that the introduction of the Western modes of thinking in the Asiatic societies, in the twentieth century, requires a formidable effort under the pressure of dire necessity.[23]

The respect that Jaspers and Toynbee display in regard to advances toward truth in past cultures is in fact "mixed with a sometimes surprising disrespect for phenomena which do not easily fit into the constructions on which the two thinkers have settled. . . . [T]heir inclusions and exclusions bear the signature of willfulness." In order to make their respective cases, Voegelin claims, Toynbee excludes Judaism from "the representative assembly of 'higher religions'; Jaspers courteously admits the prophets, but in his turn excludes Christianity from 'validity' for all mankind."[24] That is to say, both scholars selectively describe the past in pursuit of their various agendas.

In volume 4 of *Order and History*, Voegelin then reflects more generally on the tendency of scholars, even while claiming objectivity with respect to empirical data, to fashion the past in a way that is to their own liking—to submit to a "monomaniacal desire to force the operations of the spirit in history on the one line that will unequivocally lead into the speculator's present." In so doing they deploy considerable ingenuity in dealing with "obstreperous facts" that will not fit the agenda being pursued:[25]

When the Hermetical writings, erroneously supposed to be ancient Egyptian texts, became better known in the West, toward the end of the fifteenth century, a movement of human-ist thinkers placed Moses and the Bible farther down on a line of spiritual evolution that starts from the wisdom of Egyptian priests. The movement lasted for centuries. . . . When Chinese sources became known in the West, Hegel forced the spirit to start its march through history from China, while Egypt and Israel tumbled down the time-line into the Persia that con-quered them. When ethnographic materials accumulated and became fashionable, the "primitives" moved to the head of the line and originated the Communism that would ultimately issue into the dream of Marx and Engels. And when the Mes-opotamian excavations struck the West with their great dis-coveries, pan-Babylonian historians were ready to construct a new history of cultural diffusion from the origin of culture in Babylon.[26]

According to Voegelin, Jaspers falls into the same pattern in his treat-ment of the epoch of spiritual outbursts that he calls the axial age:

In order to elevate the period from 800 to 200 B.C., in which the parallel outbursts occur, to the rank of the great epoch in his-tory, Jaspers had to deny to the earlier and later spiritual out-bursts the epochal character which in their own consciousness they certainly had. In particular he had to throw out Moses and Christ. The construction did not seem to make sense. If spiritual outbursts were to be recognized as the constituents of meaning in history, the epiphanies of Moses and Christ, or of Mani and Mohammed, could hardly be excluded from the list; and if they were included, the axis-time expanded into an open field of spiritual eruptions extending over millennia.[27]

Voegelin acknowledges that Jaspers might try to avoid this criti-cism by arguing that the earlier and later outbursts had only regional, not universal, importance; and, strangely, Voegelin himself does not explicitly seek to refute this argument, even though it is entirely uncon-vincing with respect to world religions like Judaism, Christianity, and Islam. Nevertheless, Voegelin does say very explicitly, "There was no axis-time in the first millennium B.C."[28] It is an imposition on the past by modern scholarship.

Subsequent Writers

We close out this chapter by looking at the work of three subsequent authors. First, writing in 1994, Stefan Breuer re-examines key cases of claimed axial transformations precisely in terms of the alleged contrasts between the two levels of order, the transcendental and mundane, that are typically ascribed to the axial age. The result is, to quote Arnason, "a more sceptical account of the Axial Age, a much more qualified interpretation of the break with archaic cultural patterns, and a very restrictive model of radical axiality."[29] As we turn to the conclusion of Breuer's essay itself, in fact, we find a stark dismissal of the "mystification" of the Jaspers thesis. It is no *mystery*, he says, but a *coincidence* that India and China, at around the same time and as the power of the state grew, went through changes in their political and symbolic structures. It is no mystery, but also no coincidence, that the Near East was not marked earlier than it was by analogous changes. It is no coincidence, either, that such changes did occur later in the peripheral zones of the region. It *is* a coincidence, however, that these latter steps forward were contemporary with the "transcendental breakthroughs" in India and China. Breuer concludes,

> Insofar as one does not level off the differences between these different variations; insofar as one takes into consideration that there were also such breakthroughs outside these time periods; insofar as one does not lose sight, finally, of the fact that regressions and "twists and turns" followed most breakthroughs; insofar as one takes into consideration all this, there is no reason to refuse to this accumulation of coincidences the term that Jaspers bestowed upon on it: Axial Age.[30]

In other words: so long as we do not adopt Jaspers' opinions, there is no harm in retaining his terminology. This is far from a ringing endorsement of Jaspers' work.

Secondly, even while accepting the Jaspers thesis as fundamental in his book on *Stages of Thought*, Michael Barnes acknowledges that various preaxial developments in different cultures "prefigured" the later search for a single ultimate reality. Among these were the fourteenth-century BCE pharaoh Akhenaten's elevation of the sun god to supremacy in Egypt and Zarathustra's (Zoroaster's) development of the notion of Ahura Mazda as a single ultimate God.[31] Barnes notes that Zarathustra is argued by "some" to have lived at the end of the second millennium BCE, but this understates what is, in fact, a scholarly consensus that he did live around 1000 BCE.[32] Zarathustra was, of course, one of Jaspers' axial thinkers. The question that arises here is whether it is really true (as Barnes claims) that Akhenaten and Zarathustra prefigure an empirically verifiable axial age. Do they not perhaps represent evidence instead that there is something quite problematic about the notion of an axial age as a discrete entity beginning in the ninth century BCE and separable from what precedes it?

Finally, Gananath Obeyesekere's interest in *Imagining Karma* (2002) lies in comparing three eschatologies: "The rebirth doctrines of small-scale societies in various parts of the world . . . ; those in the Buddhist, Jaina, and other religions that flowered in the Ganges valley around the sixth century B.C.E.; and those of the Greeks of the Pythagorean tradition of roughly the same period." He embraces Jaspers' (and Eisenstadt's) thought when talking about "ethicization": "the processes whereby a morally right or wrong action becomes a religiously right or wrong action that in turn affects a person's destiny after death. Ethicization deals with a thoroughgoing religious evaluation of morality that entails delayed punishments and rewards quite unlike the immediate or this-worldly compensations meted out by deities or ancestors." These processes, Obeyesekere claims, are intrinsic to the axial age. Yet he is also keenly aware of the huge differences between religions like Buddhism and religions like Zoroastrianism, Christianity, and Islam in their approach to such matters, and he tells us that "the unique feature of Axial Age development in Indic religions is that their thought took a direction that ethical prophecy did not."[33] In other words, these so-called "axial" transformations were really very different from each other.

The problems with the Jaspers thesis noted by these authors have not, however, prevented the popularization of the thesis by others, as we shall see in the next chapter.

3

PROCRUSTES AND HIS BED
Mutilating the Facts to Fit a Theory

... whatever might have been thought able to lodge both Confucius and Isaiah was, from the start, strictly a Procrustean bed.

—James Montmarquet,
"Jaspers, the Axial Age, and Christianity"

I wish that she had not relied so heavily on the Jaspers myth.

—Diarmaid MacCulloch, "The Axis of Goodness,"
on Karen Armstrong

Two writers more than any others have probably been responsible for the popularizing of the Jaspers thesis: John Hick and Karen Armstrong. In this chapter we shall explore their presentations of the thesis and note the serious problems that arise. In their midst we shall set a more academic contributor to the discussion, Robert Bellah, and explore his ideas as well.

JOHN HICK

John Hick is a believer in the axial age, although he emphasizes that it did not represent

a clean break with the past but had been prepared and antici-
pated by earlier movements and has since always been qualified by elements of pre-axial religion persisting within each of
the great world traditions and within the secular societies of
today. The inevitable danger in identifying and naming this
immensely significant transition of some two and a half millennia ago is that it may thereby be made to appear more dramatic
and sharply delineated than it must have been at the time.[1]

These are helpful cautionary words. Hick also alerts us (more inadver-
tently) to one of the most striking difficulties of the axial age hypothesis, and one to which Voegelin had already drawn attention, although
remarkably few other people interested in the axial age ever explicitly
mention it. The difficulty is that this allegedly world-transforming
phase of history—in which "all the major religious options . . . were
identified and established . . . [such that] nothing of comparably novel
significance has happened in the religious life of humanity since"[2]—lies
before the rise of both Christianity and Islam. Yet these are the two religions that have arguably changed the world more than any others and
that certainly, currently, have by far the greatest numbers of adherents
worldwide. The axial age is also a period of history that lies well *after* the
time in which Jews themselves have traditionally identified their most
fundamental religious roots—the period of the exodus from Egypt.

Hick is aware of this problem, so he tells us that we may only say
what he has just said "with certain qualifications." We must understand
the rise of Christianity and Islam "as major new developments within
the prophetic stream of Semitic religious life." We must reckon that
although Judaism had a prior history, "the distinctive Jewish understanding of God, and the ways in which this understanding became
embodied in a tradition, were formed very largely by the great prophets
and biblical redactors of the axial period."[3] However, when one's overall
theory about intellectual and religious history involves such enormous
qualifications, surely the time has come to question whether the theory is driving the evidence or the evidence the theory. It is simply not
true that all the major religious options were identified and established
during the so-called axial age.[4] This is so whether or not one accepts
Hick's particular argument that Judaism is "very largely" a product of
the axial age. I myself see no reason to accept Hick's assertion on this
point.[5] This being so, I see two hugely significant religions with deep

roots prior to the axial age (Judaism and Zoroastrianism) and two others with deep roots after it (Christianity and Islam).[6] Hick does not then help his own case by acknowledging that in preaxial India we already find movements "that were to provide the setting for the great religious breakthroughs of the axial age. . . . The ideas of Karma and reincarnation were developed within this less cultic and more mystical stream from which the Upanishadic philosophy was later to emerge."[7] This is a very significant, axial-like "stream"—in the allegedly preaxial world.[8]

Sheldon Pollock summarizes well the question that arises from the kind of approach adopted by John Hick:

> If the synchrony [of Axial-type developments in different cultures] is "mysterious" enough, as Jan Assmann seems to suggest, to require extending the epoch so far back as to encompass Pharaonic Egypt, or, as implied by others, to require extending it so far forward as to encompass Islamic Iraq or even the twelfth-century "renaissance" in northern Europe . . . then even the mystery of synchrony vanishes and the Axial Age stretches out so as to be more or less coextensive with premodernity.[9]

ROBERT BELLAH

A tension similar to the one found in Hick's writing is evident in Robert Bellah's 2005 essay "What Is Axial about the Axial Age?," which later became the foundation for the introduction to the sixth chapter of his 2011 book, *Religion in Human Evolution*. In fact, Bellah has enormous difficulty in answering his own question with any degree of plausibility. He clearly *believes* in an axial age; he begins his essay by referring to it as a reality of "the middle of the first millennium B.C."[10] In describing it, however, he cannot refrain from referring not only to developments in Greece, China, India, and Israel but also to Christianity and Islam, which are certainly not products of the first millennium BCE. He acknowledges, moreover, that "Eisenstadt's emphasis on the distinction between transcendental and mundane has been questioned in the case of China" (and Greece) and that, in discussing the axial age, "it is all too easy to read in our own presuppositions or to take one of the four cases (usually Israel or Greece) as paradigmatic for all the others." He looks for a theoretical framework in which to place the axial age, then, "that will help us avoid these pitfalls as much as possible," and finds it in Merlin Donald's account of the evolution of human culture through various stages: episodic, mimetic, mythic, and (most recently) theoretic culture.[11] For Bellah "the axial breakthrough was essentially the breakthrough of theoretic culture in dialogue with mythic culture as a means for the 'comprehensive modeling of the entire human universe.'"[12]

Yet it becomes clear as we read his account that Bellah does not, in fact, see these stages of culture as merely sequential. Narrative (myth) remains the way in which we understand our lives, "one of our two basic ways of thinking. . . . Mythic (narrative) culture is not a subset of theoretic culture, nor will it ever be. It is older than theoretic culture and remains to this day an indispensable way of relating to the world." Elsewhere in the essay, indeed, he has already told us both that "the old unity of God and king was broken through dramatically in every case" in the axial age and yet that this unity was also reaffirmed in the new axial formulations (e.g., in the notion of kings ruling by divine right). This is not, it seems, the radical discontinuity in history that the notion of an axial age demands. It raises a particular question, indeed, about Bellah's dismissal of the Akhenaten revolution in Egypt as being only a *precursor* of the axial age, and not itself axial, for he dismisses this revolution precisely because Akhenaten's religion "reaffirmed the archaic unity of god and king"[13]—which is exactly what is reaffirmed in the allegedly "new" axial formulations! There is significant confusion at this point in Bellah's argument.

In my view, the real significance of the Akhenaten case is, in fact, that it represents another invitation to reconsider the whole axial age hypothesis, as Egyptologist Jan Assmann's work on the rise of monotheism indicates. Picking up on discussion about transcendent and mundane spheres, Assmann notes that "the first instance of the transposition of an idea or institution from the earthly sphere involving the social and political to the transcendent sphere of the divine, which is the hallmark of 'axiality,' is found in third millennium Egyptian ideas about the judgment of the dead at the court of the god Osiris."[14] This is a "breakthrough" into a kind of transcendence, although Assmann does not like this favorite word of axial age advocates. Another breakthrough of an axial nature in Egypt is to be found in the rise of personal piety, which created a direct relationship between a deity and a worshipper outside the official orbit of cult and temple, analogous to earlier relationships between patron and client, king and official. Such piety finds its first expression in Egypt in the fifteenth century BCE and flowers in the period after Akhenaten,[15] who was an axial figure in other respects, in that he "was the first in the history of mankind to apply the distinction between true and false to religion, the same distinction that later led to a transformation of 'axial' dimensions in the form of biblical monotheism. He was also the first to formulate the principle of exclusive monotheism, namely, that there be 'no gods but god.'" Israelite monotheism, in turn, "involves the transference of the political institutions of alliance, treaty and vassaldom from the mundane sphere of politics to the transcendental sphere of religion." This is a distinction between religion and politics of profound importance for later ages, although Assmann (like Bellah) acknowledges that the "axiality" of this distinction has not meant that subsequent history is bereft of examples where the two spheres have been reunited.[16]

So where is the radical discontinuity that the notion of an axial age demands? The question becomes even more pressing when we also read in Bellah that the impact of theoretic culture upon the societies that define the axial age—Greece, Israel, China, and India—was by no means uniform. All four are first said by Bellah "to exemplify or at least approach the capacity of theoretic culture for 'second-order thinking,' the capacity to examine critically the very foundations of cosmological, ethical and political order." The weak qualifier "or at least approach" is important, because Bellah goes on to tell us that the significance of theoretic culture was quite different in Greece than in India or China, and that "formal theoretic developments seem virtually absent in ancient Israel."[17] In *Religion in Human Evolution*, in chapter 6, he acknowledges further that "to the extent that we have made theory, second-order thinking, the criterion of axiality, Israel remains a problematic case." This is because "thinking about thinking . . . was not an Israelite concern." The need, then, to accommodate Israel leads in *Religion in Human Evolution* to a significant retreat from theory as the criterion of axiality: "In our quest to understand what makes the axial age axial, we will need to look, surely, at the emergence of theory wherever it arises, but we must also look at the possible transformation of older cultural forms into new configurations, and at the social consequences of such transformations."[18] So is theory the criterion of axiality, or is it not?

Similar confusion arises in *Religion in Human Evolution* with respect to Bellah's discussion of Greece, in chapter 7. Here he first tells us about "the axial moment provided by Greek tragedy," which is nevertheless "an axial moment that is still almost entirely mimetic and narrative, only latently theoretic." If it is only latently theoretic, how is it axial? Later he tells us that theory begins in Greece with a poem written by Parmenides. We immediately assume, then, that this is the axial breakthrough. But this is not so: "The enigmatic nature of Parmenides's poem, its combination of mythic imagery, divine revelation, and rational argument . . . would seem to limit its axial implications." Thus we have a moment in Greek tragedy that is axial even though it is only latently theoretic, and a moment in Greek philosophy which is plainly theoretic, but not fully axial. Parmenides, claims Bellah, supplies only the tools necessary for the axial breakthrough, the completion of which is found in the work of Plato and Aristotle. Yet just a few pages later it is "Socrates and Plato . . . [who] signify the completion of the axial transition in ancient Greece." Plato does so even though he "kept the mimetic and mythic aspects of tradition along with the theoretic." Aristotle is not mentioned here in the task of "completion," and when he is later discussed, it is actually as a *postaxial* thinker.[19] So when was the axial breakthrough, what made it so, and who was involved?

It is entirely unclear, in all of this, how Bellah's adoption of Donald's theoretical framework has helped him to ground the idea of an axial age any more securely than his predecessors. It still looks like a theory in pursuit of a firm empirical foundation. Bellah himself suggests toward the end of his essay that "deep comparison of the four cases [of axial breakthrough] is an as yet unfulfilled requisite for further progress in understanding the Axial Age."[20] He is no doubt thinking already of his later book, which does indeed engage in such a deep comparison. Unfortunately, as my comments above already suggest, nothing in this (in many ways excellent) book makes it any easier to believe in an axial age. Indeed, the more it focuses attention on the particulars of each of the four axial cultures discussed therein, the more the axial age hypothesis is seen by the careful reader to suffer that well-known death by a thousand qualifications. What we are dealing with, I fear, is a Procrustean bed—a preexisting structure into which the data are said to fit, when in fact they do not.[21] As Peter Wagner puts it, "The 'classical' model of the Axial Age hypothesis appears to project upon the past."[22]

KAREN ARMSTRONG

This lack of careful attention to empirical historical data that we encounter in the work of Jaspers and others, such that the theory comes to drive the interpretation of the data rather than vice versa, is particularly evident in the work of Karen Armstrong. Here I begin to anticipate more obviously a discussion to which I shall return in a later chapter—a discussion of the way in which the mythmakers who are the focus of this book *distort the content of ancient traditions*, and particularly the biblical tradition, in their pursuit of (what turns out to be) a fictional past.

A Short History of Myth

In her *Short History of Myth*, for example, Armstrong offers us an exceedingly curious reading of the biblical text of Genesis in pursuit of the thesis that some ancient people saw the rise of civilization in the period 4000–800 BCE as a disaster: "The biblical writers saw it as a sign of the separation from God that had followed the expulsion from Eden . . . the first man to build a city was Cain, the first murderer; his descendants invented the civilised arts."[23] It should go without saying, however, that the fact that civilization follows Eden, chronologically, so far as Genesis is concerned, cannot of itself be taken as an indication that its authors thought of civilization as such in a negative way, and nothing in broader biblical tradition suggests that biblical authors ever did.[24]

Then again, in telling us about the axial age, Armstrong claims that all the axial movements "were acutely conscious of the suffering that seemed an inescapable part of the human condition." If she means to suggest by this that few people had noticed suffering beforehand, that is hardly likely to be true, since there was so much of it around. If she means, however, that *reflection* on suffering and what it means was new to the axial age, this is also untrue. In his essay on the biblical book of Job in the *Anchor Bible Dictionary*, James Crenshaw describes a number of preaxial texts resembling Job—a book Armstrong later references in her *Great Transformation* (chapter 5) under her axial theme of "suffering (c. 600–530 BCE)." Crenshaw's texts include (from Egypt) *The Admonitions of Ipuwer*, *The Dispute Between a Man and His Ba*, and *The Eloquent Peasant* ("all dating from the 12th Dynasty [1990–1785 BCE]"); and (from Mesopotamia) *Man and His God* (second millennium) and *The Babylonian Theodicy* (c. 1100 BCE).[25]

Further, Armstrong claims that all the axial age sages "taught their disciples to look within themselves for truth and not to rely on the teaching of priests and other religious experts. Nothing should be taken on trust, everything should be questioned, and old values, hitherto taken for granted, must be subjected to critical scrutiny."[26] I leave it to others to comment on this statement from the point of view of axial movements outside ancient Israel. As for the Hebrew prophets of the eighth to the sixth centuries BCE, however, this is a woefully inaccurate, wildly mistaken account of what they were about. It sounds more like what a modern Western intellectual might think that *she* is about. Certainly no biblical text is cited in justification of her claim here.

The *Short History of Myth* is a small book with large defects. I have drawn attention to only a few, touching on the Bible and the ancient Near East. Simon Goldhill, professor of Greek literature and culture at the University of Cambridge, described still other faults in a strongly worded review in the *New Statesman* in October 2005:

> She has produced a book that will make any anthropologist embarrassed or angry. . . . Armstrong locates the origins of our myths in the Paleolithic period, and traces their developments in the Neolithic period. Since there is not one scrap of evidence for any mythic tale in either period, this history does no more than develop its own myth about the distant past. Indeed, it is all-too-familiar a pattern: a fictional account of the past, told to make sense of the present. Unless I have missed some deep irony (a satirical exposé of our fantasies about the past, perhaps?), Armstrong has been extremely misguided in the conception and production of this book.[27]

The Great Transformation

The same lack of careful attention to particulars is also found in *The Great Transformation*, where early in the book we once again meet the idea that we are dealing with an identifiable axial age in which there was a common vision—all evidence to the contrary (including biblical evidence) notwithstanding. Is Armstrong entirely unconscious in these opening pages of the many particulars that are problematic for her perspective? She is not. This is evident in the qualifications that appear from time to time in her text. Thus, "most" (not all) of the axial philosophers had no interest whatsoever in doctrine or metaphysics; "most" (not all) of them refused to discuss the transcendent dimension at the core of their being. The reality is, however, that these qualifications are never allowed to affect the totality of what is said about the group. Her description of "the Axial sages," as a group, is not affected at all by what is acknowledged either implicitly or explicitly to be the reality in particular cases. If it turns out, then, that a number of unequivocal assertions of monotheism in the Bible might be problematic for her own statements regarding metaphysics and transcendence, these biblical statements are simply alleged to be very few in number (and therefore, we assume, not worthy of notice). Indeed, some of them are said to possess a "stridency . . . [that] departs from the essential spirit of the Axial Age." It is Armstrong, of course, who gets to define the essential spirit of the Axial Age, apparently simply by asserting what it is. Elsewhere she refers to the "consensus of the Axial Age, [which] is an eloquent testimony to the unanimity of the spiritual quest of the human race."[28] A consensus is asserted, even though it is quite obvious from what she herself tells us that a consensus *did not exist*.

It is in this context that she makes a particularly extraordinary assertion, not about the fact of the consensus, but about its efficacy: "The Axial peoples all found that the compassionate ethic worked." Why exactly we should believe this is never made clear. In fact, what exactly she *means* by it is never made clear. What *is* clear is that we are *supposed* to believe in this ideal age of wonderful ideas and practice. We are supposed to believe in it even though it turns out slightly later in Armstrong's introductory pages that axiality is only present in the axial age from time to time, and in different measure and style, among the different axial civilizations. We are supposed to believe in this axial age even though (it turns out) Jaspers was mistaken about the dates for some of his key axial figures, which remain "speculative." But no matter: "Despite these difficulties, the general development of the Axial Age does give us some insight into the spiritual evolution of this important ideal,"[29] and so the book proceeds.

It proceeds through many twists and turns that I do not need to rehearse here. Among the axial figures that we visit along the way is the biblical Job. The book of Job is alleged by Armstrong to show that some among the Israelite community of the sixth century BCE had lost all faith in God.[30] This reading of Job is, to put the matter very mildly, unlikely to correspond to what the authors of the book meant to say by it. Ultimately she arrives back where she began: generalizing. At their core, "the Axial faiths share an ideal of sympathy, respect, and universal concern. . . . Regardless of their theological 'beliefs'—which, as we have seen, did not much concern the sages—they all concluded that if people made a disciplined effort to reeducate themselves, they would experience an enhancement of their humanity."[31] At least with respect to *biblical* faith, I do not believe for one moment that those who produced its literary tradition thought of the "enhancement of humanity" as the primary calling of the human person. Nor do I believe for a moment that they thought that self-discipline and re-education were the primary means of arriving at the salvation of which they thought they knew. The entire way in which Armstrong conceives of reality at this point in her book would have been alien to them.

The problematic nature of Karen Armstrong's engagement with data in *The Great Transformation* has been noted more than once in print by other readers. Writing in the *New York Times* in 2006, John Wilson calls her reading of Job, for example, "obtuse. . . . [S]he projects her own modern sensibility onto the text, assuming that it reveals a crisis of faith in the exiled Jewish community rather than an affirmation of God's unfathomable sovereignty."[32] He goes on to characterize *Great Transformation* as "a story of the Fall in which the serpent in the garden is none other than that old devil, Organized Religion," setting it in the context of other stories about a "Fall," told by those who are not persuaded by the Genesis version: "Whatever form they take, such stories invariably recall a time of exceptional human flourishing, explain how the glory fled and suggest that we might recover at least some of it today."

Writing in the same year in the Manchester *Guardian*, in the review from which my second epigraph to this chapter comes, Diarmaid MacCulloch, professor of the history of the church at the University of Oxford, tells us that he does not believe in the axial age, calling the Jaspers thesis "a baggy monster, which tries to bundle up all sorts of diversities over four very different civilisations, only two of which had much contact with each other during the six centuries that (after adjustments) he eventually singled out, between 800 and 200 BCE." In Armstrong's hands, the axial age gets baggier still, MacCulloch claims—even though he warms to various aspects of her book, which he describes as "rich and deeply felt." Nevertheless, in his view she "constantly awards brownie points or black marks to thinkers or cultures for their nearness to or remoteness from 'the axial vision,' which may suggest that the axial vision hypothesis doesn't explain very much at all."[33]

CONCLUSION
THE DEATH OF THE AXIAL AGE

There never was such an entity as an axial age, I suggest. It is a construct that has little to say for itself from the point of view of actual historical data. Only inattention to the past, or indeed downright misrepresentation of it, provides the theory with the air that it needs to breathe in order to stay alive. Jaspers himself tells us that "an accumulation of historical analysis must increasingly clarify the thesis, or else it must be abandoned."[34] We should take him at his word and abandon it—or, better, put it to death so that it cannot find its way back to us.

4

HAPPY HUNTING (AND GATHERING)
The Dark Green Golden Age

Any civilized religion, including Christianity, Judaism, Islam,
Buddhism, Confucianism . . . is a religion of occupation . . .
civilized religions lead people away from their intimate connection to the divinity in the land that is their home and toward the
abstract principles of this distant religion. How differently would
we relate to trees if instead of singing "Jesus loves me" . . . we,
those of us who live in Tu'nes, were to sing "I love these red-
woods, and they love me."

—Derrick Jensen, *Endgame*

Dark green religion . . . increasingly shapes the worldviews and
practices of grassroots social activists and the world's intelligen-
tsia. It is already important in global environmental politics. It
may even inspire the emergence of a global, civic, earth religion.

—Bron Taylor, *Dark Green Religion*

Many of the authors I have discussed in chapters 1–3 embrace the notion
of an axial age by way of advocacy. They not only believe in the *existence*
of such an age; they look back to it for *inspiration*, and they ground in
it proposals about our human and planetary future. This is not the case
with all the believers, however. It is not the case, for example, with

John Zerzan. Writing in his *Twilight of the Machines*,[1] Zerzan's concern is that we should all find our way back home, and the axial age is not in his view a helpful signpost on the road.[2] Instead, it is one of the very reasons why we find ourselves *so far away from home* in the first place.

What has happened to us, to take us so far away? Zerzan's answer, in brief, is civilization. Before civilization, human beings lived in societies organized around natural and cosmological cycles. These Paleolithic societies were founded on "the principle of relatedness [that] is at the heart of indigenous wisdom: traditional intimacy with the world as the immanent basis of spirituality."[3] Then came the Neolithic agricultural revolution and the domestication of animals. For a while the nascent Neolithic civilization coexisted with traditional societies. But with the axial age, civilization took an iron grip,[4] "a deeper hold on the human spirit, world-wide." The language itself indicates very clearly that whereas for others the advent of this civilization was a good thing, for Zerzan it was not: "The whole heritage of sacred places, tribal polytheism, and reverence for the earth-centered was broken, its rituals and sacrifices suddenly out of date." There was a breakdown of community as individual religious identity developed, and a breakdown also in the human relationship with the earth. We may note the significance of the language here: this is no axial break*through* but only a break*down*. For Zerzan, the personal now took precedence over the social, the human over the natural. In fact, "the Axial religions offered 'salvation,' at the price of freedom, self-sufficiency, and much of what was left of face-to-face community."[5]

Just as the axial age advocates have a present and a future agenda in mind as they describe its wonder, so too does this detractor as he describes its failings. Today's reality of unfolding disaster, Zerzan suggests, "has a lot to do with the relationship between religion and politics—and more fundamentally, with accepting civilization's trajectory as inevitable." There is a direct line to be drawn from the axial age to our present moment; that is where our current troubles in modernity originate, in our "escape from community, and from the earth." Only if our direct relationship with the world is restored "can a spirituality that matters return. Religion, a contrived human projection . . . is no substitute." We must "allow ourselves to see what has happened to us, including the origins of this disaster." We must abandon the industrial mode of existence, looking for guidance on the way ahead to "those who have continued to live spiritually within nature" (i.e., native peoples).[6] On this reading the axial age is a fateful, destructive age. We must recover a more authentic way of being. Central to the recovery is the renewed embrace of preaxial spirituality, which is assessed in Zerzan's thinking very differently than in (say) Jaspers' thinking. This reflects a broader debate among students of religion "between those who consider nature religions to be religiously or politically primitive, regressive, or dangerous, and those who laud such religions as spiritually perceptive and ecologically beneficent."[7]

Consider, then, the very real difference between a writer like Karen Armstrong and a writer like John Zerzan. While Armstrong welcomes to some extent the insights of indigenous religion, the axial age is for her the period to which we need to turn for help in saving our planet. It was pivotal to the spiritual development of humanity, and we must return there for guidance, because we have never surpassed its insights. We need to recover the axial ethos, in fact. That is where we find the spirituality of empathy and compassion we need, even though later generations have tended to dilute it. For Zerzan, on the other hand, this is *precisely* the wrong period of human history to which to return for help. We must rather go back to the period of harmony with nature, before civilization and before axial religion, whether the religion is Abrahamic or Vedic. There we will find the spirituality we need, as we encounter our hunter-gatherer ancestors in the state of nature and uncorrupted by civilization.

In this chapter we shall consider others who, like John Zerzan, look for their inspiration to a much earlier era of human history than the axial age—to the era known to archaeologists as the Paleolithic Age—in order to gain their sense of who they are, where they should be heading, and what they should do next. This Paleolithic Age (the Old Stone Age) stretches from the earliest moments when humans began to use primitive stone tools down to about 8000 BCE. It comes to an end at the same time as what geologists call the Pleistocene epoch (commonly referred to as the Ice Age), which gives way to the Holocene epoch in which we now live. Archaeologically, the geologists' Holocene epoch begins with the Neolithic Age (the New Stone Age), marked by the rise of farming and the domestication of animals. The Neolithic Age in turn comes to an end with the widespread use of metal tools (the Bronze and Iron Ages). It is to the Paleolithic Age, then (on this view), that we should turn for wisdom in our present moment of need, and not to the later period in which civilization and world religions arose.

Our point of entry in discussing this second "new story" about the world will be Bron Taylor's recent and helpful book, *Dark Green Religion: Nature Spirituality and the Planetary Future.*

DARK GREEN RELIGION

Taylor uses the phrase *dark green religion* to refer to "religion that considers nature to be sacred, imbued with intrinsic value, and worthy of reverent care"[8]—the kind of religion that has been spreading rapidly around the world in recent times and has become beloved by so many. It is dark, he thinks, both in the sense that there is in it a *deep* shade of green concern and also in the sense that it carries a degree of threat. A key figure in moving toward an understanding of the phenomenon, Taylor suggests, is the eighteenth-century French philosopher Jean-Jacques Rousseau, who in Taylor's view articulated many of the key ideas now typically found in dark green religion:

> a critique of materialism as a distraction from what makes people truly content or happy, namely, intimate contact with and open-hearted contemplation of nature . . . ; a belief that indigenous peoples lived closer to nature and were thus socially and ecologically superior to "civilized" peoples and from whom civilized people had much to learn; a conviction that people in the state of nature and uncorrupted by society have a natural predisposition toward sympathy and compassion for all creatures and a corresponding conviction that a good society would cultivate and not destroy such affections; and finally, belief in an expansive self in which one's own identity includes the rest of nature and a felt unity with and empathy for it.[9]

Rousseau, Taylor continues, also articulated strong criticisms of "revealed" religions, believing that "they distort human societies into forms that detract from the freedom and well-being of all natural beings." These are criticisms that "have continued to gain traction ever since."[10]

Dark green religion manifests itself in four main types, Taylor claims in his second chapter. All of them possess historical antecedents. They comprise two variants each (naturalistic and supernaturalistic) of animism, on the one hand, and Gaian earth religion, on the other.[11] As an exemplar of the supernaturalistic stream Taylor cites (among others)

Gary Snyder; as exemplars of the naturalistic stream (among others), Jane Goodall and James Lovelock. Snyder is the author of the 1974 Pulitzer Prize–winning *Turtle Island*. The primatologist Goodall was designated in 2002 as a United Nations Ambassador for Peace. Lovelock is best known for his Gaia theory about the biosphere as a self-regulating organism (Gaia being the Greek goddess of the earth). The eighteenth-century ideas noted by Taylor above are, I observe, reflected among the various people cited in his second chapter in various ways. They are reflected when Snyder, for example, associates monotheistic religion with the (unnatural) formation of centralized governance and the national state, noting that monotheism and authoritarian nationalism appear to belong together.[12] They are reflected when the same author asserts that "the world's dominant theistic religions are inferior to nature religions and place-based spiritualities."[13] They are in evidence again when Lovelock tells us that "our religions have not yet given us the rules and guidance for our relationship with Gaia. The humanist concept of sustainable development and the Christian concept of stewardship are flawed by unconscious hubris."[14] Religion, conceived in this way, is not good for us.

In chapter 3 Taylor "examines some of the critical figures . . . who were responsible for the emergence and subsequent strength of dark green religion in North America."[15] These are people like Ralph Waldo Emerson, Henry David Thoreau (who once said that "he had much to learn from Indians . . . but nothing to learn from missionaries or even from Christ"),[16] and John Muir. Taylor discusses not only these important figures but also their predecessors. His chapter 4 deals with "radical environmentalism," of which one typical characteristic is, according to Taylor, "its critique of Abrahamic anthropocentrism, which is believed to separate humans from nature." This critique appears not just in nonfictional writing but also in fiction like Marion Zimmer Bradley's novel *The Mists of Avalon* (1983), in which "druidic, earth-revering, and goddess-worshipping pagans" resist "an invading patriarchal, nature-destroying, Christian culture."[17] Taylor identifies another novel, Daniel Quinn's *Ishmael* (1992), along with its sequel, as articulating "the most prevalent cosmogony found within radical environmental subcultures":

> A gorilla named Ishmael . . . [teaches] that the fall from the Edenic state of harmony with nature was precipitated by the domestication of plants and animals and the concomitant

advent of agriculture, which went hand-in-hand with world-denigrating religions. Totalitarian agricultures then spread globally, destroying biologically diverse ecosystems and animistic foraging cultures wherever they went. In Quinn's reading, the religions of imperial agricultures, whether Abrahamic or Vedic, all promise divine rescue *from* this world, instead of promoting feelings of reverence toward and belonging to nature.[18]

It is in the context of this discussion of radical environmentalism that Taylor himself briefly mentions John Zerzan as one of those who have been promoting "'anarcho-primitivism,' a type of radical environmentalism that, like most forms, considers foraging societies superior to agricultural and pastoral ones; but it adds an anarchist and primitivist ideology that envisions and seeks to hasten the collapse of nation-states and all industrial civilizations." Another of the anarcho-primitivists is Derrick Jensen, whose thinking we shall consider further below. While Jensen is certainly open to employing violence in pursuit of his goals, many other radical environmentalists do not envisage doing so. Taylor's final example in chapter 4 is Paul Watson, the cofounder of Greenpeace, who he thinks has produced "the best extant insider-penned summary of radical environmental religion." Watson begins this summary "by urging people to abandon the world's dominant religions, claiming that they promote and justify violence, bigotry, and anthropocentrism and focus 'exclusively on the superiority and divinity of the human species.'"[19] He proposes instead a new story, a new myth, and a new religion, replacing anthropocentrism with biocentrism: "An acceptance of interspecies equality allows a sense of planetary belonging."[20] In Watson's view, many indigenous peoples already possess stories of the kind required in this present moment.

After an interesting fifth chapter on the themes of dark green religion as they show up in the spirituality of surfing (which in 2005 Brad Melekian suggested "may be the next world religion"),[21] in chapter 6 Taylor turns his attention largely to film, including the documentaries of David Attenborough and David Suzuki. For Suzuki (whom we shall consider further below) "scientists and indigenous peoples have similar insights regarding ecological interdependence, and . . . they often share common ethical and spiritual perceptions about the intrinsic value and sacredness of nature." Indigenous peoples are indeed "the best remaining stewards of . . . critically important spiritual and ecological knowledge." Chapter 7 examines dark green religion in arts, sciences, and letters as they are found represented (for example) in magazines like *National Geographic*, in New Age and neopagan literature, in photographs, and in institutions like the United Nations. Given the ubiquity of dark green religious themes, chapter 8 wonders "whether we are witnessing the emergence of a global, civic, earth religion," which Taylor refers to as "terrapolitan earth religion" (a term coined by political theorist Daniel Deudney). "Although unrecognized by the Parliament of World Religions," Taylor writes in his conclusion, dark green religion "is as widespread as most religions, more significant than some, and growing more rapidly than others . . . most critically, it has a coherent set of beliefs that its adherents find compelling. Rather than rescue from this world, it offers an enveloping sense of belonging to the biosphere, which is considered sacred."[22]

Unless I have missed it, Taylor does not once use the term *axial age* in his book, nor does he refer to Jaspers. I do not know whether any of those with whom he engages in the book, other than Zerzan, use this language or refer to Jaspers either. What is very clear, however, is that the *concept*, if not the language, of the axial age is reflected everywhere in the writings and other communications of the exponents of dark green religion. Which *are* the dominant, world-denigrating religions, after all, that promise rescue from the world and are now so useless to us who are faced with saving the world? They are the religions arising immediately or secondarily from the "axial age breakthroughs," with their emphasis on transcendence. Which *are* the people groups who still tell truer stories about the world than we modern people do and without whose spiritual and ecological knowledge we cannot manage? They are the preaxial tribal peoples not yet entirely assimilated into axial reality. They are especially those peoples who are the most "primitive," that is, who are preagricultural and prepastoral. The *concept* of the axial age, at least, is just as crucial to those narrating the past in this way—and envisioning the future and deciding what to think and do in the present in connection with the future—as it is to John Zerzan. The specific language of the axial age is simply one way (Zerzan's way) of referring to a widely shared idea about when our human problems began—that is, with civilization and with world religions. Prior to this era, it is widely assumed by dark green religionists, there was something very like a golden age of human existence. It was a dark green golden age, in fact, in which people possessed more truth than their descendants and lived in ways that were more authentic, world affirming, kind, and peaceable than those of which their descendants have proved themselves capable.

DAVID SUZUKI

Bron Taylor provides us with a helpful overview of dark green religion and of the story, broadly speaking, that its adherents tell about the world. Something of the diversity of person and perspective in the "movement," however, as well as the commonality, is communicated if we delve further down into Taylor's narrative and retrieve for further inspection two very different kinds of adherent to the myth. In a moment we shall consider the thinking of Derrick Jensen. First, though, we shall interact with the work of David Suzuki.

Suzuki's body of work is perhaps best accessed by way of his recent short book *The Legacy*, which rehearses much of what he has written before.[23] The book is based on a 2009 lecture that was self-consciously written to sum up all that Suzuki had learned in his lifetime. His pressing interest is in the environmental crisis that presently confronts us, and in what needs to change if we and other creatures are to survive and flourish in the future. Our evolution as a superspecies, he suggests, has led us to a place in which our human relationship with the planet has changed markedly, relative to what has gone before. "Human beings," he tells us, "have become such a powerful force that we are altering the life-support systems of the planet." These alterations are then explored through the lens of what ancient Greek philosophers held to be the four elements of the material universe (earth, air, fire, and water), in the midst of commentary on population growth and declining biodiversity. "The crisis is real, and it is upon us."[24]

What is required going forward, suggests Suzuki, is that we develop a sense of place in the world and a reverence for nature, such that economics and politics take their lead from nature and function *in correspondence to* nature, rather than *dominating* nature. This requires some reflection on the place of science in our modern world, since "science itself must . . . take some of the blame for the loss of reverence and respect for nature" that is a feature of our contemporary scene. This is so because "science . . . obliterates wonder and awe, the sense of the sacred or the profane, when it focuses on parts of nature—a powerful methodology called reductionism"—rather than upon the whole.

We need to look at the world through different eyes, seeing the big picture and understanding that we ourselves "are deeply embedded in and utterly dependent on the generosity of the biosphere." Returning to the four elements of the material world, Suzuki reminds us that we ourselves *are* air and water and earth and fire. All creatures on earth are our kin. We need to learn to look at the world in just such a way, becoming more human by learning to love other species and to live "in balance with the sacred elements." We shall then be able to begin to imagine a new way of living—"creating a vision of what must be." In turn, this will determine how we must act. Suzuki paints his own vision of the future in concluding the book, urging "sustainability within a generation." He ends by expressing great confidence in our human capacity "to rediscover our home, to find ways to live in balance with the sacred elements, and to create a future rich in the joy, happiness, and meaning that are our real wealth."[25]

As elements of this brief description suggest (e.g., we are to "rediscover our home"), Suzuki's understanding of the present and his vision of the future are integrally bound up with a particular understanding of the past. We do not need to depend on our own resources, he tells us, as we seek to develop an appropriate mind-set and appropriate practices. We can (and should) draw on the resources with which our ancestors provide us. For

> it used to be understood that we have a sacred duty to pass on to future generations a world that is as rich as or richer than the one we came into. . . . For most of our existence, people knew that we were deeply embedded in nature and that our very survival depended on nature's generosity. We understood that everything in the world was connected, that what we did had repercussions, and that therefore every act was laden with responsibility.[26]

We used to understand all this, back into the mists of time and down through history until fairly recently. To illustrate the point, Suzuki cites the traditional practice of North American aboriginals who, when considering an important decision, thought about the implications for the seventh generation after them. These modern survivors of an earlier time provide us with a bridge back to it—to a time before the point in history when "in a moment of explosive change, we lost our way, forgot the narrative that reminded us of who we are, why we are here, and where we belong." So it turns out that "perhaps we don't need to find a new story but to rediscover an old one."[27] This old story is still told, by aboriginal or traditional peoples all over the world, and we need to pay attention to their wisdom—as the UN document *Our Common Future* (1987) also urges us to do, claiming that "these communities are the repositories of vast accumulations of traditional knowledge and experience that links humanity with its ancient origins. . . . [We] could learn a great deal from their traditional skills in sustainably managing very complex ecological systems."[28] It is not entirely clear from *The Legacy* precisely when Suzuki thinks that the "moment of explosive change" occurred, when "we lost our way." Some of the statements he makes in his earlier writings might lead one to believe that he is thinking only of the onset of modernity in the sixteenth and seventeenth centuries,[29] and not of an earlier period. The Bible can appear in Suzuki's earlier writings as itself an exemplar of *traditional* religion (e.g., in *The Sacred Balance*),[30] and a religion like Christianity can avoid thoroughgoing criticism prior to its seventeenth-century incarnation in Europe (in *The Wisdom of the Elders*).[31] Yet even in *The Wisdom of the Elders* Suzuki and his coauthor Peter Knudtson acknowledge that some of the roots of the problematic scientific mind-set "descend into the deeper tilth of ancient Judeo-Christian and Greek thought."[32] In *The Sacred Balance*, moreover, Suzuki contemplates many centuries in which not just Judaism and Christianity but perhaps also Hinduism and Islam allegedly moved away from their "earliest forms . . . [which] presented an animated, integrated world similar to that of traditional worldviews" and developed into later forms that did not present such a world.[33] He also acknowledges in the latter book that many thinkers blame Plato and Aristotle for the problem. When we get to the distinctions drawn in *The Wisdom of the Elders* between "native and scientific knowledge about nature,"[34] it is monotheism *as such* that is associated with the scientific mind, along with related realities like the distinction between sacred and profane realms. It is specifically the Judeo-Christian tradition that is in view, in fact, with its emphasis on human dominion over nature, on unilinear rather than cyclical time, and on ultimate consequences for sin. The point is explicit in two quotations upon which Suzuki draws. The first, from a Swedish historian of religion, radically differentiates "the Western religious dichotomy between a world of spiritual plenitude and a world of material imperfection, a dualism pertaining to

Christian and Gnostic doctrines" from the holistic religion of American native peoples. The second, from a Tewa Indian and anthropologist, stresses that "Indian tribes put nothing above nature. Their gods are a part of nature, on the level of nature, not supra-anything."[35]

In the end, then, it is monotheism that is the problem. Echoes of the axial age resound, even though Suzuki does not use that language (to my knowledge) anywhere in his writing. It is the period prior to this problematic age upon which we must focus if we are to move safely ahead—a period to which we gain access through aboriginal peoples of the present time. When they have vanished, "their body of price-less thought and knowledge, painstakingly acquired over thousands of years, will disappear forever." It is not simply wishful thinking, Suzuki claims, to believe in this connection between the present and the past. He himself tells us in *The Wisdom of the Elders* that he has "no rose-tinted illusions about the 'noble savage,' but those who deny that living remnants of an ancient aboriginal worldview still persist, speak in igno-rance." The connection is real. Later in the book Knudtson and Suzuki return to the same point, referencing Callicott: "The idea that Native worldviews are steeped in genuine environmental wisdom is not, he insists, some sort of 'neoromantic invention' or a return to guilt-ridden, Western notions of 'noble savages.' On the contrary, it arises from a clear-eyed recognition of indigenous societies' sense of *relationship* with the natural world, from which flow very different environmen-tal values and responsibilities." For Knudtson and Suzuki, indigenous nature wisdom foreshadows a certain kind of future "by its historic precedent of sustaining a long-term ecological equilibrium with the natural world."[36] The golden age exists. We ignore it at our peril.

DERRICK JENSEN

Derrick Jensen's thinking is well exemplified in the first of his two vol-umes entitled *Endgame*, which is subtitled *The Problem of Civilization* and dates from 2006.[37] In this book Jensen seeks to persuade the reader, by way of anecdote, example, and argument, of twenty premises. The first and most fundamental is that "civilization is not and can never be sustainable"—especially industrial civilization. Immediately we detect an important disagreement with David Suzuki, who is optimistic about the ability of civilized peoples to attain (or recover) sustainability. For Jensen, this is a delusion. He quotes with approval fellow activist George

Draffan: "The only sustainable level of technology is the Stone Age." That is the level of technology with which human beings have lived for most of our existence. This all changed with the rise of cities and city-states in the ancient world—groups of people "living more or less permanently in one place in densities high enough to require the routine importation of food and other necessities of life." These urban dwellers created an ever-increasing region of unsustainability surrounded by an increasingly exploited environment. This is the beginning of civilization, which has been marked throughout history not just by the exploitation of the environment but also (according to Lewis Mumford) by "the centralization of political power, the separation of classes, the lifetime division of labor, the mechanization of production, the magnification of military power, the economic exploitation of the weak, and the universal introduction of slavery and forced labor for both industrial and military purposes." Our current, modern, and industrial version of civilization is thus founded, like its predecessors, on violence. This violence is directed not least against traditional communities, whose destruction is required for civilized peoples to acquire from their land the resources they need. Our way of living, Jensen suggests, would collapse very quickly were it not for persistent, ongoing, and widespread violence—violence against other human beings and violence against the natural world, revealing itself in exploitation and degradation. This violence, however (where it is even noticed), is widely accepted, because from birth "we are individually and collectively enculturated to hate life, hate the natural world, hate the wild, hate wild animals, hate women, hate children, hate our bodies, hate and fear our emotions, hate ourselves. If we did not hate the world, we could not allow it to be destroyed before our eyes. If we did not hate ourselves, we could not allow our homes—and our bodies—to be poisoned."[38] We live within an unsustainable civilization, most of whose citizens are insane. We inhabit a culture driven by an urge to destroy life and to embrace death. According to Jensen, however, we cannot see it, precisely because we have been inducted *into* it from birth and still live *within* it.

Is this civilization redeemable? It is not. We need to face "the intractability of this culture's destructiveness." The sixth of Jensen's twenty premises is that it "will not undergo any sort of voluntary transformation to a sane and sustainable way of living. If we do not put a halt to it, civilization will continue to immiserate the vast majority of humans and to degrade the planet until it (civilization, and probably the planet) collapses." Because every city-state in ancient times, and now the entire globally interconnected industrial economy, relied and relies on imported resources, exploitation and violence *must* inevitably continue. Those engaging in the economy *must* remain impervious to appeals to conscience, humanity, and decency. They *will* do so, not least because the powerful are more interested in increasing their own personal power, and that of the state, than they are in human and nonhuman wellbeing. Power is more important than life: "Begging government and industry to stop destroying the planet and to stop killing people the world over is never going to work. It can't." Therefore, we ourselves must stop it. In fact, "the longer we wait for civilization to crash—or before we ourselves bring it down—the messier will be the crash, and the worse things will be for those humans and nonhumans who live during it, and for those who come after." To be active in undermining civilization is therefore to be virtuous. To be passive in the face of it is to risk being rightly blamed by future generations, who will ask: "Why did they not take it down?"[39]

Like David Suzuki's vision of the present and the future, Derrick Jensen's understanding is integrally bound up with a particular perspective on the past. It is a past in which human beings and their immediate evolutionary predecessors lived sustainably in their world, markedly refraining from destroying their habitat. This was certainly true in North America, which when civilized people arrived "was rich with humans and nonhumans alike, living in relative equilibrium and sustainability."[40] For Jensen, the hunter-gatherer society is the ideal, when measured not only by the criterion of sustainability but also by the criteria of available leisure time, social equality, and food security (meaning that no one goes hungry).[41] These traditional peoples lived in harmony with nature and, indeed, in accordance with the cycles of nature. They lived in "ahistorical" cultures, "in the moment" and profoundly in a *place* in which there was "divinity present in every rock, plant, animal, river, and raindrop, as well as every moment of every being's life." Their religions, emerging from the land itself, taught them "how to live in place." These were not only prosperous societies but also peaceful ones, since "indigenous warfare . . . is a relatively non-lethal and exhilarating form of play." The idyllic life that Jensen has in mind is well represented by his particular idea of the Yurok of Oregon and California, whom he pictures by the Klamath River fishing, hunting, gathering, performing rituals, building their homes, and playing. They live sustainably, "using their own energy, energy gained from eating, metabolizing."[42]

Then came civilization. Domesticators enslaved plants, animals, and land to the agriculturalist and all of us to the process of agriculture. Sky gods were invented, divorced from the earth, and kingship was lowered from heaven to the earth so that the divine king could superintend the life of his slaves in the city-state. The cyclical was replaced by the linear, and the notion of progress was instituted (based on the changes made to the world by those with the power to make them). The world was transformed—most unfortunately: "Had somebody snuffed out civilization in its multiple cradles, the Middle East would probably still be forested, as would Greece, Italy, and North Africa. Lions would probably still patrol southern Europe. The peoples of the region would quite possibly still live in traditional communal ways, and thus would be capable of feeding themselves in a still-fecund landscape." Civilization was *not* snuffed out, however—neither then nor later. And although each human being still has the potential to become the sort of adult who can live sustainably on a particular piece of ground, each one comes under immense pressure, from childhood onwards, to become civilized rather than to remain human. It is, for Jensen, as stark as that: to be human or to be civilized.[43]

Just as the critique of civilization is stronger in Jensen than in Suzuki (and the solution with respect to our current crisis much more radical), so too is his critique of axial age religions much less ambiguous. All the religions associated with civilization—among them (explicitly) Christianity, Judaism, Islam, Buddhism, and Confucianism—are criticized as religions of occupation (as we see in the first epigraph to this chapter). All are transposable religions that do not emerge from the particularities of any landscape; all "lead people away from their intimate connection to the divinity in the land that is their own home and toward the abstract principles of this distant religion." Jensen's main target, besides Buddhism, is Christianity, which lies at the root of the story of Western civilization that Jensen regards as "the story of the reduction of the world's tapestry of stories to only one story, the best story, the real story, the most advanced story, the most developed story." This is a faith that legitimates the conquest of all other cultures and indeed the planet, since its primary texts include one that commands human beings to subdue the earth and have dominion over it. It is a faith whose primary texts teach us that rape is acceptable, whose God's home is not primarily of this earth, whose God cannot provide us with a workable this-worldly ethic, and whose worshippers think that the killing of the planet is to be encouraged because it will hasten "the ultimate victory of God over all things earthly, all things evil." This Christian faith is a faith whose apostles include Paul, "a domineering asshole . . . [who] used Christianity as a vessel for his pre-existing rigidity." It is a faith whose central symbol, the cross, is a symbol of dying to the flesh so that we can be reborn in the spirit—a symbol that suggests that the world is "an evil place, a vale of tears where the enemy death constantly stalks, a place that is not and can never be as real as the heaven where bodies . . . no longer exist, a place that can never be home."[44] This Christian faith is a faith thoroughly bound up, in the past and in the present, with American nationalism and militarism[45]—thoroughly bound up with civilization, which is "killing the world." Such religion, proclaims Jensen, must be left behind, along with the civilization associated with it. We must believe, rather, that "the material world is primary . . . that spirit mixes with flesh . . . we cannot rely on Jesus, Santa Claus, the Great Mother, or even the Easter Bunny."[46] For Jensen, then, we must leave civilization behind us, and return to an earlier time. Indeed, we *will* sooner or later return to an earlier time, whether we want to or not, for civilization cannot ultimately survive.

AN APPRECIATION . . . AND ANOTHER QUESTION

The story of the dark green golden age, like the story of the axial age, is evidently a popular story. It is persuasive to many to some degree, contributing significantly to their sense of who they are, where they should be heading, and what they should do next. And just as I affirmed in chapter 1 the good in much of what those who recount the axial age story have to say, so here also in chapter 4 I want to affirm the good in much of the story told by dark green religionists. I am as enthusiastic as Zerzan about "the principle of relatedness [that] is at the heart of indigenous wisdom." I am just as troubled as he is by the breakdown of human community and of the human relationship with the earth that can follow in the wake of individualized religion. I agree with the various writers with whom I have interacted above that axial age religions can be so focused on the transcendental and on escaping from present earthly reality that they neglect and even damage that reality. I am certainly open (with Suzuki) to learn what I can from the indigenous peoples who still survive, as well as from our Paleolithic past. Along with Paul Watson and Derrick Jensen, I abhor violence, bigotry, and (at least inappropriate) anthropocentrism. Above all, I am completely convinced that we human beings must change our ways, and quickly, if we are to leave a world behind us in which our children and grandchildren, along with all of God's other remaining creatures, may flourish.

With all such affirmations stated, however, this important question remains—the same question that I asked about the axial age in chapters 2 and 3. Was there ever really a dark green golden age, historically, prior to a later axial age? Or is it a myth? Bron Taylor may himself think that it is a myth, because in his report on a hearing at the Earth Summit in Johannesburg in 2002 he writes:

> The critical mythos of the hearing reflected dark green themes, including the conviction that most people used to live sustainably but that a fall from an earthly paradise occurred, resulting (variously, depending on the speaker) from agriculture, hierarchy, patriarchy, monotheism, technology, and capitalism, all of which disconnect us from nature and produce greed, indifference, and injustice. The globalization process itself was said to destroy traditional and sustainable agro-ecosystems. This involved . . . an increasing and sacrilegious commodification of life . . . which in turn depended on the theft of intellectual property from indigenous people and the destruction (if not theft) of their lands.[47]

It is noble to stand against greed, indifference, injustice, and the sacrilegious commodification of life, and to advocate for sustainable agro-ecosystems. It does not ultimately help such causes, however, to tell untrue stories about the past. So is the dark green story true? Or is it false?

5

HARD TIMES IN THE PALEOLITHIC
Constant Battles and Unequal Rights

There is nothing wrong with seeking generalizations; indeed, this is part of the obligation of a scientist. But generalizations should not mask the underlying variability.

—Robert Kelly, *The Foraging Spectrum*

The common assumption is that only when . . . increasingly more complex societies spread, and in particular when European civilizations came to dominate much of the world through colonizing, was warfare introduced (and induced) to the far corners of the earth. . . . Such an impression misses the essence of human history.

—Steven LeBlanc, *Constant Battles*

Where is the evidence of an earthly paradise just prior to the rise of agriculture, hierarchy, patriarchy, and monotheism? Why should we believe in such a dark green golden age, just prior to "civilization," in which humans lived in harmony with nature, possessing untold wisdom that we moderns do not possess about how to live in the world and a natural predisposition toward sympathy and compassion for all creatures?

In this chapter and the next I shall argue that there is no good reason to believe in such an age. We certainly lack *direct* evidence that this is how the world was back then. Faced with this deficit in direct evidence, advocates of the dark green golden age typically resort to what they regard as good indirect evidence. They propose that we can learn about the distant past by way of observation and analysis of *modern* hunter-gatherer societies, both in our immediate present and in the more recent documentable and recoverable past. There is little reason, however, to think that this belief is well founded. But even if it *were* well founded, the lives of these modern "primitive peoples" would not suggest anything like an Edenic dark green golden age in the Paleolithic past. If the lives of these peoples suggest anything about the distant past, it is certainly not *that*.

THE INFORMATION DEFICIT AND THE COMPARATIVE METHOD

In chapter 3 we noted Simon Goldhill's criticism of Karen Armstrong's attempt to locate the origins of our myths in the Paleolithic period and then to trace their developments in the subsequent Neolithic period. The problem is that there is no evidence for any mythic tale in either period. This case illustrates a general truth: in speaking about the distant human past, we are speaking about periods of human history for which there is a pronounced information deficit. About the Paleolithic era, which concluded around ten thousand years ago with the end of the last Ice Age, we know very little. We possess no written documents dating from this era, and we possess only a relatively limited amount of archaeological evidence. We do know from the latter that by the end of the Paleolithic era these distant ancestors of ours had discovered fire, had domesticated dogs, had learned to trap salmon, and had begun to produce art (e.g., cave paintings). They had certainly learned to fashion tools, of wood, stone, and bone. But we know not much more than that.[1] We are little better off when it comes to the Neolithic era that followed the Paleolithic and was marked by the development of farming, by the more widespread development of animal domestication, by larger and more permanent settlements, and ultimately by the appearance of pottery. Again, we lack written documents.[2] We know relatively little about Neolithic societies, beyond these very basic facts.

This information deficit was already confronted by those nineteenth-century European thinkers whose ideas about the prehistoric past and how to access it have proved so influential. How might it be possible, they asked, in the light of (what was at the time even *more*) limited archaeological evidence, and in the absence of written sources of information, to reconstruct human prehistory? How might we fashion out of the fragments of the prehistoric past a coherent story of human progress toward modernity? The answer they arrived at was the comparative method, which, "stated simply . . . took existing cultural (and biological) diversity in the world and turned it into an evolutionary sequence. Different peoples represented different stages in humanity's march to perfection."[3] Lewis Henry Morgan, for example, described world history in terms of seven eras—three of "savagery," three of "barbarism," and then finally civilization. He thought it possible to identify contemporary peoples in terms of how far they had advanced along this time line.[4]

The criteria employed by these thinkers to make this kind of determination included the marital practices of a people (monogamy was ranked higher than polygamy), their authority structures (patrilineal was ranked higher than matrilineal descent), and their religion (monotheism was ranked higher than polytheism). Once positioned on the time line, a people group could then be used as a window into the past—the past from which (especially northwestern) Europeans had emerged into the modern light of day. It was thought that modern hunter-gatherers or foragers, in particular—people who obtain most or all of their food from wild plants and animals, rather than from farming or from domesticated animals—could provide a "window" into the Paleolithic period, since they represented "relic populations," left over from this earlier era of our human past. As the reader will already have deduced, these relic populations were not, in the nineteenth century, favorably regarded. They were considered as "intellectually incapable of developing the technology needed to permit a sedentary existence . . . [and without any] concept of private property, a sure sign of arrested moral and intellectual development."[5] These were primitive societies that needed to be civilized.

Times change, of course, and the mood of the 1960s and 1970s was different in some quarters in the West from that of the late nineteenth century. Confidence in "progress" was much diminished, and so was satisfaction with the Western way of life: "Westerners searched for an alternative way of life, where material possessions meant little, where people lived in harmony, where there were no national boundaries,"[6] and where people cared more about their environments. It is perhaps not surprising that in this new context we find the beginnings of a radical re-evaluation of the past by anthropologists in which the nineteenth-century understanding is turned on its head.

An important event in this process of re-evaluation was the "Man the Hunter" conference hosted by the University of Chicago in 1966, out of which emerged a number of interesting ideas. Among these were the notions that the hunter-gatherer societies known to us are really gatherer-hunter societies (in that plant food rather than meat is the focus of subsistence), that they are egalitarian and peaceable, and that they consciously keep their populations sustainably low, in harmony with their environment. Their "failure" to own individual property (including territory) is, in fact, a virtue, *born* out of confidence that the environment will meet their needs and *resulting* in a lack of conflict over resources. Their "failure" to develop elaborate culture is not due to circumstances (i.e., the need constantly to look for food) but is a consequence of their lack of materialism. Transporting these ideas into the past, we are then able to reconstruct Paleolithic human society as somewhat idyllic in comparison to modernity. Since it would have been a society based on sufficiency rather than surplus, it would have demanded of its members, who lived in a bounteous environment, relatively little work and would have allowed them significant leisure time. It would have been a society living in harmony with itself and with its surroundings—in Marshall Sahlins' words at the conference, a truly "affluent society." In this new reading of the past, the rise of agriculture, previously seen as a liberating force in human history that enabled people to escape the harsh demands of primitive life, inevitably comes to be understood as a negative development. Agriculture is embraced by hunter-gatherers only under duress, so that they "leave their life of leisure behind, become agriculturalists, and work for a living."[7]

This revised late twentieth-century view of the prehistoric past is obviously entirely different from the late nineteenth-century view. The latter is premised on the notion of an upward, the former on a downward, movement through history, culminating in modernity. "Primitive" peoples are correspondingly either the unfortunate folks whom progress left behind or the fortunate folks who lived in a golden age before regress set in. The late nineteenth-century view is the eventual outflowing of a confident European Enlightenment and before that of the thought of Thomas Hobbes in his *Leviathan* (1651), who in his thirteenth chapter famously characterized the "natural" human life outside of civilized society as "solitary, poor, nasty, brutish, and short."[8] We must escape this condition, claimed Hobbes, by means of a social contract, subjugating nature through reason and method. We find ourselves as we begin, in this Hobbesian story, in a traditionally Christian "fallen state," and we must move onwards from there.

The late twentieth-century view, in contrast, is the eventual outflowing of currents in European intellectual life during the Renaissance, where the myth of an ancient golden age played a centrally important role.[9] These currents eventually flowed out into the European romanticism of the eighteenth and nineteenth centuries, which arose in reaction to the Enlightenment, to the scientific rationalization of nature, and ultimately to industrialization. Romanticism involved the revaluing of emotion and imagination, of the spontaneous and the natural, and of folk art and ancient custom. Those who followed this line of thinking argued that human beings in the state of nature (i.e., before they are civilized) are far from being solitary brutes. In fact, they possess sympathy, and indeed benevolence, toward their fellows. These writers often referred to the native peoples of the world that Europeans were then encountering, especially in North America, as examples to illustrate their point. Indeed, they frequently compared native society favorably to civilization, which they described as being in various ways corrupt and unjust.

We find this view already expressed, for example, in Marc Lescarbot's *Histoire de la Nouvelle France* (1609) and reflected in John Dryden's 1672 play, *The Conquest of Granada*, where the hero, Almanzor, asserts,

> I am as free as Nature first made man
> 'ere the base Laws of Servitude began
> when wild in the woods the noble Savage ran.[10]

We find it also in Baron de Lahontan's somewhat fictional but popular travelogue, *New Voyages to North America* (1703), in which (in the words of Paul Hazard) "science and the arts are the parents of corruption. The savage obeys the will of Nature, his kindly mother, therefore he is happy. It is the civilized folk who are the real barbarians."[11] In due course this widely shared habit of romanticizing and idealizing the precivilizational past came to be characterized (by those who objected to it) as promoting "the myth of the noble savage," picking up on the language of Dryden (and before him Lescarbot). In this myth we find ourselves as we begin in a kind of Christian "garden of Eden," we "fall" then into civilization, and it is civilization from which we must save ourselves (if we can).[12]

For all that differs in these nineteenth- and twentieth-century views, however, it is important to understand that they share a notable premise. They may disagree violently about exactly *what* modern "primitive peoples" tell us about the prehistoric past; nevertheless, they certainly agree in assuming that these peoples do in fact give us reliable *access* to the prehistoric past. But is this a safe assumption? Robert Kelly reminds us that "long before anthropologists arrived on the scene, hunter-gatherers had already been contacted, given diseases, shot at, traded with, employed and exploited by colonial powers, agriculturalists, and/or pastoralists. The result has been dramatic alterations in hunter-gatherers' livelihoods." All such peoples "live physically and socially on the outskirts of societies different from their own. They interact with these societies through trade, marriage, and employment, and have done so for some time."[13] That is to say: these are *modern* peoples, even if they have not (yet) availed themselves (or been able to avail themselves) of all that modernity has to offer. They are not prehistoric peoples living in splendid isolation from the rest of the world in the present and (therefore) connecting us inevitably, in their eternal changelessness, with a distant past. In some cases, indeed, their hunter-gatherer lifestyle has been (re-)adopted as a relatively recent phenomenon, in order to escape such modern realities as conscription and taxes, or simply to make a political statement. There is, it seems, no unbroken connection with the past at all.

This recognition, Kelly tells us, has led some anthropologists to abandon the "generalized foraging" model of the 1960s and 1970s and to replace it with the "interdependent" or "professional primitives" model. They have done so in recognition of the fact that modern hunter-gatherers remain so not because of a philosophy about nature but "because it is economically their most viable option in their very restricted circumstances."[14] Proponents of this model avoid using modern "primitive peoples" to reconstruct prehistory; they are much more concerned about understanding the reality of their lives as people enmeshed in contemporary political and economic realities.

If we were to grant for the sake of argument, nevertheless, that the people groups in question might be able to tell us *something* about the distant human past in which our ancestors no doubt lived lives *somewhat* similar to theirs—what would that something be? Would the lives of modern "primitive peoples," both in our immediate present and in the more recent documentable and recoverable past, suggest anything like an Edenic dark green golden age in the Paleolithic period?

AN AGE OF PEACE?

Would they suggest, for example, that back then people were capable, in a way that modern human beings are not, of living in peace? In the fifth chapter of his important book *Constant Battles: The Myth of the Peaceful, Noble Savage*, archaeologist Steven LeBlanc examines the reality of early hunter-gatherer societies (he prefers the term *forager*) through the lens of three extensively studied people groups: the !Kung of the South African Kalahari Desert, the Aborigines of Australia, and the Inuit of the Arctic. In Australia, first, "archaeology reveals burials with evidence of violent deaths and even massacres, and specialized weapons useful only for warfare have been found. . . . There are ethnographic accounts of indigenous people fighting other indigenous people."[15] Second, historical accounts of the seventeenth to the nineteenth centuries clearly reveal bands of !Kung in conflict with each other and with other indigenous people groups, and rock art predating European settlement depicts battle scenes. "There is no evidence that the !Kung or their related groups at the time these early historical records were written were living in ecological balance, nor were they peaceful." They fought each other, and they joined together to fight others, sometimes creating security zones ("no-man's-lands") around themselves. Third, "almost all the early Arctic anthropologists and explorers recorded incidences of warfare and stories about warfare among the Inuit," and the Inuit certainly possessed tools of war (including body armor). The archaeological record bears witness to "serious and deadly warfare among Arctic foragers," which could involve torture.[16] These more recent hunter-gatherer societies certainly do not provide any basis for a reconstruction of the distant past in which such societies were innately peaceable.

Indeed, the *archaeological* evidence itself from the more distant past does not suggest that such a peaceable age existed either. LeBlanc describes, for example, the European archaeological site of Dolní Veštonice, a village dating from around 20,000 years ago. It is located on a defensible hill, surrounded by a wall of mammoth bones, and mass burials of fighting-age males have been found there. He notes the various prehistoric cave sites in France (e.g., Lascaux), where we find a number of portrayals of humans being speared or otherwise dead or dying. He describes a graveyard in Egypt dating from the end of the Paleolithic period, in which were found the remains of fifty-nine people, "at least twenty-four of whom showed direct evidence of violent death, including stone points from arrows or spears within the body cavity." Moving on to the Mesolithic period, he tells us about Ofnet in Bavaria, where an entire social group was massacred, and about burial evidence from Brittany (around 6000 BCE) that suggests that about 8 percent of all deaths was due to warfare. Summing up the European situation, he states that "from very early times in Europe, there is evidence of individuals who were victims of lethal wounds, mass burials, cannibalism, massacres, and warfare depicted in rock art."[17] Some of the oldest skeletons known from North America, he adds, also show evidence of violence.

This liking for warfare among human beings LeBlanc traces both backwards and forwards from the Paleolithic period. He traces it *backwards* via the reality of chimpanzee warfare to the common ancestors of both chimpanzees and humans, noting that chimpanzees forage in much the same way human foragers do and that they fight in groups with other bands of chimpanzees.[18] He traces it *forward* to the rise of tribal farmers and then of complex human societies.[19] He discusses, for example, the tribal warfare of the New Guinea highlands, which early ethnographers in the 1960s mistakenly described as "play fighting." In reality, warfare in that region up until very recent times was endemic, with "formal battles, ambushes, and even occasional massacres going on almost continually." The fighting was nasty, with arrows smeared with excrement to cause infection in the victim. It was also deadly: 25 percent of the men and 5 percent of the women died as a result of warfare. As LeBlanc says, "this last place on Earth to have remained unaffected by modern society was not the most peaceful but one of the most warlike ever encountered."[20]

Similarly frequent, intense, and deadly warfare is documented among the next least-exposed group of tribally organized farmers, the Yanomama of Venezuela, with large buffer zones maintained between settlements in order to keep enemies at a distance.[21] Buffer zones like these were also noted in North America by Lewis and Clark in the course of their famous expedition in 1804–1806. Toward the end of that expedition, Clark observed that it was "in the country between the nations which are at war with each other [that] the greatest number of animals are to be found."[22] We shall return to this quotation, and to Lewis and Clark, in the next chapter when we think about the important "myth of general abundance" in the nineteenth-century United States and the question of ecologically wise native peoples. For the moment let us simply note that one of the reasons significant native hunting did *not* take place in some parts of the United States, with the consequence that abundant game *was* to be found in those areas, is that various native peoples were at war with each other. Therefore, to venture into the buffer zones between their territories was to risk conflict. Paul Martin and Christine Szuter quote one writer from a slightly later time (1839) as stating that the American native peoples "recognize certain districts, where buffalo usually abound, as common hunting and war ground, where various tribes roam at will, subjecting their conflicting rights to the tests of strength. Between the tribes there is perpetual warfare."[23] This is warfare among traditional enemies, of course; it did not begin to be a reality only after contact with Europeans. The native peoples of North America fought fiercely among themselves long before they met the Europeans.[24]

LeBlanc cites all this evidence to dispel the misconception that human beings are

> peaceful by nature and . . . have been so for millions of years. This notion assumes that for much of human history people lived in nonviolent societies and maintained pleasant, helpful, symbiotic relationships with their neighbours . . . [and] war was not the norm or a constant threat. Popular belief also holds that only after the development of "civilization," or highly complex societies, did things begin to change.[25]

Popular belief is mistaken, he goes on to say (in the second epigraph to this chapter); people in the past "were in conflict and competition most of the time."[26] The conflict and the competition are indeed connected. There has been warfare from the beginning, because there has been from the beginning no world peopled by inherent conservationists—as we shall see in our next chapter. We have never lived in a world in which people manage and take care of their environments, making sure that they never misuse or overexploit anything and consequently enjoying a world in which there is plenty for everyone. The myth of the ecologically wise ancestor is deeply bound up with the myth of the peaceable ancestor. Both are aspects of what LeBlanc refers to as the romantic myth of the noble savage. The reality is that it is not just our present time that is marked by "constant battles and heedless gobbling up of the nearest natural resources." This was also true of the distant past.[27] Moreover, lack of peace is not just a feature of *inter*tribal relations in ancient societies; it is a feature of *intra*tribal relations as well. Thomas Headland tells us that, in *Sick Societies: Challenging the Myth of Primitive Harmony* (1992), "[Robert] Edgerton rejects the idea that tribal peoples lived generally in great harmony, health, and happiness and in balance with their stable environments; instead, he argues that such cultures are full of dysfunctional practices that keep people in misery and maladapted to their environments."[28] Headland continues,

> The 1993 symposium "Crime in Prehistory" . . . lent support to Edgerton's argument. . . . [T]he meeting's program chairs said that its participants "challenge[d], as simplified and distorted, views that portray prehistory as peopled exclusively by members of happy, peaceful communities, living in harmony with each other and with their environment. Instead, panelists describe[d] numerous examples in the prehistoric record of conflict over resources and episodes of environmental degradation, including deforestation, soil erosion, soil depletion, and mass overkilling of herds."[29]

There are, in sum, no good reasons to consider the Paleolithic Age in human history to be an age of peace.[30] To the question of whether it was an age marked by ecological wisdom we shall return shortly.

AN AGE OF EQUALITY

May we at least claim that it is likely, on the analogy of modern hunter-gatherer societies, that the Paleolithic was an age of equality?

In his extensive examination of extant hunter-gatherer peoples, Kelly reserves his eighth chapter for an examination of egalitarian and nonegalitarian hunter-gatherers. He acknowledges that the unreflective undergraduate mind probably already has a default picture of hunter-gatherer groups like the Ju/'hoansi of the Kalahari: "small, peaceful, nomadic bands, men and women with few possessions and who are equal in wealth, opportunity and status." Even the undergraduate mind knows in its better moments, however, that the situation is much more complicated than this. It knows, for example, that there are hunter-gatherer societies that are nonegalitarian and "whose elites possess slaves, fight wars and overtly seek prestige." These latter societies are often unhelpfully referred to as *complex*, as opposed to *simple*. They have often been regarded, indeed, as exceptions to the "simple" rule—as products of atypical environments that are rich in resources. Kelly notes, however, that archaeologists have continued "to discover evidence of prehistoric nonegalitarian hunting and gathering societies in many environments."[31]

It seems, therefore, that nonegalitarian hunting and gathering societies have always been with us. They include the peoples of North America's Northwest Coast, some people groups in California, the Ainu of Japan, and the Calusa of Florida. Such peoples tend to have high rates of violence. Violence is indeed culturally sanctioned and appears to be related to status difference between men. It also expresses itself in "warfare and raiding for food, land, and slaves [which] were probably fairly common in places such as the Northwest Coast . . . before European contact." There is no equality of access to food and no equality between men and women. The women are viewed as "secondary to men, as a means to increase household production, or as a means to manipulate social relations with other villages."[32]

These societies differ markedly from those relatively egalitarian societies that people often have in mind when they describe foraging peoples. The word *relatively* is important, however. Even in "egalitarian" hunter-gatherer societies, members do not have equal *amounts* of such goods as food and prestige; they only have equal *access* to such goods. And it is not that everyone "buys in" to the egalitarian ideal—as if we were dealing with people groups in which all members were ideologically and morally pure and worked hard to maintain equality. What makes many hunter-gatherer societies egalitarian is not an absence of people who attempt to "lord it over" others, but communal strategies to undermine such people. Even then, individual autonomy can, in practice, be lost in the course of giving prestige to, say, a particularly good hunter—the beginning, perhaps, of the transformation of an egalitarian into a nonegalitarian society. Even where societies are designated egalitarian, the reality of male-female equality on the ground is particularly questionable in many cases:

> Even in that classic egalitarian society, the Ju/'hoansi, women appear to have autonomy and control only when they demand it. . . . Ju/'hoansi men do about two-thirds of the talking at public meetings and act as group spokespersons more frequently than women. . . . [I]n domestic conflicts Ju/'hoansi women are far more commonly the victims than are men; the same holds true for Australian Aboriginal women.[33]

Kelly begins the conclusion to his chapter in the following way:

> The study of hunter-gatherer societies offers the opportunity to study a range of human sociopolitical organizations: from egalitarian to nonegalitarian, from societies where men and women are relatively equal, to those where they clearly are not. We are still far from an understanding of what conditions engender egalitarianism or hierarchy, but it is certain that though egalitarianism is not a natural condition of humanity, neither is hierarchy.[34]

There are, in sum, no good reasons to consider the Paleolithic Age in human history to be an age characterized by equality. Certainly the analogy of modern hunter-gatherer societies provides us with no grounds for confidence that it was.

6

Ecologically Noble Ancestors?
Why Spiritual People Don't Necessarily Look after Their Living Space

. . . the appearance of balance between traditional native groups and their environment has more to do with low human population densities, lack of markets, and limited technology than it does with any natural harmonious relationship with nature.

—Michael Alvard, "Testing the 'Ecologically Noble Savage' Hypothesis"

It is . . . important to surrender the image of the aboriginal peoples living in idyllic harmony with host ecological systems, at least if by that is meant living in a way that conformed to current notions of ecological propriety.

—Thomas Neumann, "The Role of Prehistoric Peoples in Shaping Ecosystems in the Eastern United States"

Would the lives of modern "primitive peoples" suggest anything like an Edenic dark green golden age in the Paleolithic period? In chapter 5 we considered this question from the perspective of peace and equality. In this chapter we shall consider it from the perspective of ecological wisdom and useful religion.

AN AGE OF ECOLOGICAL WISDOM?

Would the lives of modern "primitive peoples" suggest that long ago people were capable, in a way that modern human beings are not, of living in harmony with nature? Are we safe in assuming, on the analogy of modern hunter-gatherer societies, that our prehistoric ancestors took care not to exceed in population the carrying capacity of their environment or to damage the earth and its various animal populations?

The Native Peoples of Amazonia

The native peoples of Amazonia have often been depicted as possessing an innate conservation ethic of the sort that my questions imply. The Tukanoan peoples of the northwest, for example, forbid deforestation of the riverbanks; this has been heralded as management of the river's edge so that its resources remain sustainable. The Gorotire Kayapó have been credited with a management technique arising out of an environmental philosophy that involves the creation of "islands" of forest in the savanna of central Brazil. The Cocamilla have been portrayed as enhancing floodplain lake-fishing resources by adding manure and garbage to the lake waters to increase nutrients. In these cases and in others, however, Allyn Stearman suggests that there is, in fact, no evidence that a conservation ethic is functioning at all.[1] The "conservation" that arises is simply an accidental by-product of the main business at hand: surviving as best one can in challenging circumstances. *It is resource constraints that drive their practice, not an environmental philosophy.*

Stearman notes that the original 1983 report on the Cocamilla, in particular, states on more than one occasion that the people themselves have no conscious awareness of managing the lake. Indeed, she further notes that most of the original analyses of the indigenous practices she describes do not mention a conservation ethic in relation to the practices: "These assertions tend to come later and in an entirely different context, primarily when these cases are reinterpreted in light of the growing rhetoric concerning the role of indigenous peoples as conservationists." Over against these examples of allegedly conservationist behavior in Amazonia, Stearman cites the example of the Yuquí of eastern Bolivia, who do not face resource constraints and whose "use patterns . . . tend toward extravagance rather than conservation."[2] She notes that the Yuquí kill animals without regard to age or sex, including females with young or who are pregnant, and that they do not value animals apart from their usefulness as food. Their fishing habits are damaging from an ecological perspective, as are their patterns of harvesting fruit. Insofar as the Yuquí nowadays show more concern about conservation than they did before, they do so as a result of outside influence.

These and other cases are not exceptions to the rule, Stearman concludes "and are certain to disturb those who romanticize indigenous peoples according to their own ethnocentric perceptions of how native societies relate to nature." Those same romantics were shocked and outraged when in the early 1990s it emerged that the Kayapó were exploiting for profit the natural resources on their reserve in just the way that many nonnative peoples might do.[3] They might still have been shocked and outraged, but at least not surprised, if they had taken the time to talk with the natives themselves. Perhaps they should have listened to someone like Nicanor González, a Kuna Indian from Panama, who writes, "I don't believe that you can say that indigenous peoples are conservationists as defined by ecologists. We aren't nature lovers. At no time have indigenous groups included the concepts of conservation and ecology in their traditional vocabulary."[4] Alternatively, perhaps Brazilian Marcos Terena, president of the Union of Indigenous Nations, could have prepared them: "We are people just like you. Some of us view nature with a great sense of stewardship whereas others must perforce destroy some of it to obtain what they need to eat and pay for expensive medical treatment and legal counsel."[5]

A Particular Case: The Diamante Piro

Among the Amazonian peoples who do *not* possess a great sense of stewardship are the Diamante Piro of Peru, who have been studied by Michael Alvard. While it is certainly true, he says, that "indigenous people have an intimate knowledge of their environment, perhaps rivaling Western scientific specialists in some areas," the question remains "whether native knowledge is utilized to maintain a balance with nature, or simply to procure resources in the most efficient manner possible."[6] In the case of the Piro, Alvard argues that there is no evidence that hunting decisions are made to ensure sustainable harvests of prey. That is, no restraint is exercised in the short term to ensure viable animal populations in the long term. The Piro behave, in fact, in just the way that what he calls "foraging theory" predicts; that is, they overexploit resources whenever it is to their immediate advantage to do so.[7] Short-term interests dominate.

If restraint *were* being exercised, argues Alvard, we would expect the Piro to avoid endangered animals like the howler and spider monkeys and the tapir, as well as the cracid game birds (guan and curassow). During the shotgun hunts that Alvard observed, however, howler and spider monkeys were pursued on every occasion upon which they were encountered, and tapirs on almost every occasion.[8] The game birds were often ignored early in a hunt, but only because the hunters were waiting to see if they could kill anything better (given that shotgun shells were limited). These birds were much more likely to be pursued after half the hunt was over. In anthropological language, the Piro were subject in this case to "attack limitations." All these fauna are on the Piro's "optimal prey choice" list, in accordance with foraging theory, along with such fauna as the collared peccary, the agouti, the red brocket deer, and the capuchin monkey. These are prey that are "either large packages of calories or types that can be taken with relatively short pursuits."[9]

Like the howler and spider monkeys and the tapir, collared peccary and deer were almost always pursued on the hunts. Agoutis were only sometimes pursued, which is initially surprising in terms of foraging theory predictions but is in fact explicable in terms of different kinds of encounters between hunter and prey. On the one hand, there were encounters where an agouti saw the hunter first and fled (and was usually not pursued). On the other hand, there were encounters where the agouti was unaware of the hunter's presence; most of the encounters where agoutis were killed were of this kind. It was all a matter of efficient use of time. A combination of variable encounters and attack limitations, Alvard suggests, also explains most of the situations where capuchin monkeys were not pursued. Alvard concludes his essay by anticipating that further research on hunting practices will provide support for the idea that the appearance of ecological balance in areas where native peoples are living has more to do with factors like low population density than with any "natural harmonious relationship with nature."[10]

The Māori of New Zealand

Moving now from Amazonia to the other side of the world, we may consider the case of the pre-European Māori settlers in what is now New

Zealand, who most likely arrived there in the twelfth or thirteenth centuries CE as a population of several hundred. Foraging theory once again predicts that these settlers would exploit natural resources in ways that expended the least effort for the greatest return, with resources diminishing or disappearing in proportion to their desirability and vulnerability. That is indeed what we find in New Zealand.

These early Māori settlers did what was easiest for them in terms of survival. They hunted, and their hunting contributed, either directly or indirectly, to severe pressure on some animal populations[11] and the eventual extinction (among others) of 50 percent of the Holocene bird species present when they arrived. In the millennium prior to the Māori arrival, "there is no documented extinction of any New Zealand avian species (indeed of any vertebrate)"; but after they arrived, and before the Europeans did, New Zealand lost "nearly forty species of birds, a bat, three to five species of frogs, and an unknown number of lizard taxa." Among the birds that disappeared was the moa, which appears to have been especially targeted, but it was not the *only* target; in fact, "remains of all prehistorically extinct species of late Holocene birds have been found in at least one archaeological site, apart from two tiny wrens and two recently recognised species."[12]

Where direct predation was not necessarily responsible for extinction, there was still a huge amount of collateral damage, as predators further down the food chain lost their means of sustenance (e.g., the great eagle, which feasted on moa) and habitats were disturbed or destroyed. One of the ways in which habitats were adversely affected was by fire, the incidence of which greatly increased in New Zealand after human settlement. To what extent these fires were deliberately set by the Māori to clear ground for horticulture or to facilitate travel and to what extent they were accidental is unclear. Certainly the dense forests that burned were of no great value to them in terms of food resources. What *is* clear is that the forests of the eastern South Island of New Zealand had virtually been eliminated by around 1450 CE and that forests had also been burned out of the lower east coast of the North Island and of Hawke's Bay. In the end, it is calculated that 50 percent of New Zealand's primeval forest disappeared during the pre-European Māori period.

The further ecological consequences of both the deforestation and the loss of the large browsing birds were profound. "The nature of the pre-European Māori environmental impact was, in its early stages, almost certainly one that is typical of colonisation everywhere and at all times," Anderson suggests. "Migration into new environments releases a powerful instinct to expand as rapidly as possible, using the richest resources with pitiless energetic efficiency. Evolutionary fitness drives lineage competition in the use of unowned resources toward levels of overexploitation described as the 'tragedy of the commons.'" He concludes, "Similar changes occurred elsewhere in the Pacific Islands, in Australia, and in the Americas. They are characteristic of the entry of people into previously uninhabited and fragile environments."[13]

The Pacific Islanders

Among the Pacific Islands we may mention Rapa Nui (Easter Island), Mangaia (in the Cook Islands), and the Hawaiian Islands. Prior to colonization in the second half of the first millennium CE, Rapa Nui was a forested island providing "a varied habitat for other life forms no longer extant on the island"[14] as well as a breeding ground for more than twenty-five species of seabirds (and a smaller number of land birds). Direct and indirect human actions over time led to the removal of the forest and its replacement with grassland, as well as to the extinction of the fauna, as the human population grew to near the carrying capacity of the island. On Mangaia, also, there is evidence of significant environmental change after human colonization (around 200 CE), as the Austronesian colonists deployed slash-and-burn technology, the forests diminished, ferns and other plants replaced trees, and the fauna began to disappear. There is also evidence of overfishing. Finally, the Hawaiian Islands were extensively settled by 1200 CE by Polynesian voyagers, who quickly caused changes in lowland vegetation by clearing forest so that they could farm. In due course we see a level of extinction among birds similar to the level observed in New Zealand, as population increased and more pressure was exerted on the land.

The Native Peoples of North America

Similar patterns of profound human impact on the environment are found all over the world, from Europe to Africa and on to New Guinea. Contrary to the assumption by many people of influence, not to mention the general public, that "native North Americans had little impact on the flora and fauna of the continent,"[15] these patterns are certainly found prior to the arrival of European settlers in what are now Canada and the United States. The original native peoples in these lands were, in fact, "the ultimate keystone species who created the very ecosystem that we now consider 'natural.'"[16]

They may be implicated early on in the eradication of some thirty-five genera of mostly large animals (megafauna such as mastodons, saber-toothed cats, and giant sloths) that occurred during the end of the Pleistocene period, which coincided with their initial colonization of the New World from Asia (around 10,000 years BCE). This remains a controversial matter.[17] Even if they are not implicated in those extinctions, thereafter they certainly "drove populations of highly desirable 'target species' or 'preferred prey' to low levels, or even to local extinction,"[18] just as one would expect if a people "pursued an optimal-foraging strategy with no effective conservation practices."[19] Drawing on historical sources such as the journals of the Lewis and Clark expedition of 1804–1806, Martin and Szuter argue that "the range and numbers of surviving large animals were profoundly influenced by the activities of Native Americans well before European settlement." These animals "were abundant or scarce depending on cultural as well as environmental conditions. . . . We conclude that those parts of the continent harboring large animals in large numbers historically were either buffer zones, war zones, or, as a result of the diseases of contact, sparsely inhabited areas." That is to say, there was an inverse correlation between the presence of a significant human population and significant numbers of large animals. Clark is on record as observing, in fact (as we saw in chapter 5), that "in the country between the nations which are at war with each other the greatest number of animals are to be found."[20] Beyond warfare, the significance of disease in removing human predators and thus allowing animal (in this case fish) populations sometimes to rebound is also hinted at in this comment by a visitor to the San Francisco Bay area in 1833: "The rivers were literally crowded with salmon, which, since the pestilence had swept away the Indians, no one disturbed."[21] Abundant wildlife was found, in other words, where human beings were absent or greatly diminished in number.

None of this speaks of "conservation practices" with respect to animals on the part of Native American peoples historically. Neither does much else in the historical record. Consider the case of the buffalo. When the buffalo arrived on the plains each year, the Plains Indians would kill them in large numbers in a short period of time, often eating only the best parts and leaving the rest to decay on the ground—depending on factors like the distance to their camp and the available means of transportation. Where the geography allowed it, they were also known to stampede entire herds of buffalo over cliffs in order to get access to some of the dead for food. This is completely understandable from a human perspective, taking into account the historical moment that they occupied. "Nature" is something that only modern romantics, residing in their comfortable modern environment, can afford to be romantic about, and an understanding of the complexities of ecosystems and our own part in changing them is a fairly recent phenomenon (and even now a disputed matter). The peoples who lived in North America before the Europeans arrived clearly did not understand these complexities in a very sophisticated way, if at all, and sympathy and compassion for all creatures was not their main concern. Their main concern in the case of buffalo, for example, was to kill them and eat them when they had the chance, without themselves being killed by what were (after all) very large and aggressive animals. It was simply easier and safer to run a herd off a cliff than to try to sneak up on one individually. These hunters were not concerned so much about the waste that was created by their success as they were about the lack of food that would result from their failure. They lived in a harsh environment: wildly fluctuating temperatures throughout the year, tornadoes, flooding, predators, limited water supply in many places, and above all a lack of edible plant life. This is why the Plains Indians feasted so extravagantly when the buffalo came. They were mainly meat eaters, and buffalo represented their main supply.

It was, more or less, as simple as that. Ecological wisdom did not come into it. These peoples were not living in harmony with nature in the way that dark green religion invites us to imagine them. They were *struggling* with nature, as human beings have always had to do. That they did more limited damage to their environments in the process than modern peoples have managed has little to do with holding a different view of the world or possessing a different spirituality. It has more to do with ancient peoples' limited technology and their relatively low population numbers—populations in turn kept in check by a nature upon which technology had not yet much imposed itself. Ancient spirituality could itself *contribute* to their less-than-ecological approach to the buffalo. Believing that buffalo were, in fact, other-than-human persons, many Plains Indians also believed that buffalo escaping from a place in which they had been trapped would warn other buffalo. So even if they had more than enough meat, they would kill all the surviving beasts. Other Plains Indians believed that buffalo were created in countless numbers underground, or in a certain lake, emerging each year onto the prairie to supply their needs. If the buffalo could not be seen, it was not because of population decline or some such modern concept. It was because they had not (yet) left their point of origin. It is not easy to see how anything approaching a conservation ethic might arise out of such a belief system.[22]

The Paleo-Indians of North America changed their ecosystem, upsetting the previous "balance of nature," with respect not only to its fauna but also to its flora. They did this to such an extent that Gerald Williams can even ask, "Are there any 'natural' plant communities" in North America?[23] He asks this question against the background of substantial evidence that, for various reasons, Native Americans engaged extensively in burning their environment. This is a reality reflected in the words of the Dutch mariner De Vries in 1632, when he wrote that the American continent "is smelt before it is seen."[24] Drawing on more than three hundred studies, Williams generates a list of eleven major reasons for this burning. For example, American natives burned large areas in order to drive big game into small, unburned areas where they could be hunted more easily, or into narrow chutes or river or lakes, or over the edge of cliffs. They burned for agricultural reasons, including the harvesting of crops and to clear ground for planting. They burned to control pests (e.g., to kill poisonous snakes), to improve grasslands for big-game grazing, and to create firebreaks to protect valuable plants as well as their settlements. They also burned to deprive their enemies of cover and of building materials, to alert their allies to enemy movements, and to attack their enemies. They burned to clear trails for travel and to fell trees. Fire, it turns out, "has been the major tool that American Indians used to change ecosystems to their survival."[25] They did not simply accept the environments they found when they first entered the New World twelve thousand years ago and then seek to live in harmony with them. They adapted their environments to suit their own purposes.

The cumulative effect of this modification of the continent by fire by these first immigrants "was to replace forested land with grassland or savannah, or, where the forest persisted, to open it up and free it from underbrush. Most of the impenetrable woods encountered by [European] explorers were in bogs or swamps from which fire was excluded; naturally drained landscape was nearly everywhere burned."[26] It is these "impenetrable woods" that often feature in literature in which European explorers *depicted* America, but what they largely *found* when they arrived was "thick clouds of hazy smoke enveloping the land, grasslands reduced to charred stubble, and park-like forests clear of undergrowth."[27] This was by no means a pristine wilderness, inhabited by people striving to tread lightly on the land:

> It often seems that the common impression about the American West is that, before the arrival of people of European descent, Native Americans had essentially no effect on the land, the wildlife, or the ecosystems, except that they harvested trivial amounts that did not affect the natural abundance of plants and animals. But . . . there is ample evidence that Native Americans greatly changed the character of the landscape with fire, and that they had major effects on the abundances of some wildlife species through their hunting.[28]

The fact is that by the time European explorers arrived in North America, "millions of acres of 'natural' landscapes or 'wilderness' were already manipulated and maintained for human use, although the early observers did not recognize the signs . . . prairie and forest were to a large extent the creation of indigenous peoples."[29]

They did not "recognize the signs." They did not understand what they were looking at: an environment deeply impacted and indeed changed by its ancient inhabitants. It was also an environment already deeply impacted by the European presence itself—and this too they did not understand. They saw abundance in flora and fauna, and they interpreted this as a landscape upon which humanity had not yet impressed itself. In fact, however, this abundance itself was in some measure the consequence of European diseases decimating the native populations and removing the top predator of the previous ecosystem from its exalted position. They were not looking at the way the landscape had always been. They were looking at what the landscape had only recently become. It is out of these multiple incomprehensions on the part of the early European explorers and settlers, which were then distilled into their writings, that the romantic notion about the original character of North America emerged to become so fixed in the modern mind. And still the mistakes that they made are repeated by others in the present time. The story of the passenger pigeon, for example, is recounted often in dark green religious literature—one of many stories that are told in order to show, says Charles Kay, how "pre-Columbian America teemed with wildlife before Europeans drove that and other species to extinction."[30] But in fact, Kay continues, "it was only after European diseases decimated Native American populations, and thereby freed the mast crop [acorns and other nuts] for wildlife, that passenger pigeons irrupted to unprecedented numbers." The facts have been misconstrued, yet again, by those in dogged pursuit of a myth. Pre-European abundance is not what it seems. It is not even pre-European.

Which Kind of Age?

Our selection of people groups in this chapter has inevitably been small. However, Bobbi Low has conducted a study of the same subject using the 186-society Standard Cross-Cultural Sample—a sample composed (as the name suggests) of 186 traditional societies "stratified for geographic distribution and language group, and for which ethnographies by qualified ethnographers resident with the society for a substantial period of time are available." Her conclusions correspond to what we have already discovered. People in traditional societies "do not, at least to their ethnographers, express a widely held conservation ethic. To the contrary, in most societies, people express individual need rather than some sort of communal long-term planning." Her two main findings are that "resource practices are ecologically driven and do not appear to correlate with attitudes (including sacred prohibition) and . . . the low ecological impact of many traditional societies results not from conscious conservation efforts, but from various combinations of low population density, inefficient extraction technology, and lack of profitable markets for extracted resources."[31] In sum: *if* we were to grant for the sake of argument that the lives of modern "primitive peoples" might be able to tell us *something* about the distant human past in which our ancestors lived, it is entirely clear that they give us no reason to suppose that people back then were capable, in a way that modern human beings are not, of living in harmony with nature, of living within the population carrying capacity of their environment, and of avoiding damage to the earth or its various animal populations. Consequently (as Thomas Neumann says at the head of this chapter), it is "important to surrender the image of the aboriginal peoples living in idyllic harmony with host ecological systems."[32]

AN AGE OF USEFUL RELIGION?

We conclude our exploration of our ancient past by considering the important question of religion. Is there any evidence to suggest that the old, precivilizational religions of ancient hunter-gatherer peoples, emerging as they did from the land itself, were particularly helpful in teaching these peoples "how to live in place" (as Derrick Jensen puts it)? Were they helpful in teaching them, as dark green religionists often claim, how to live well in their land, displaying ecological wisdom, peaceableness, and equality?

Since we have already established that there is no reason to think that these ancient peoples *did* display notable ecological wisdom, peaceableness, and equality, there is of course also no reason to think that their religions particularly helped them toward these goals. We just read, indeed, that one of the two main findings in Bobbi Low's study was that "resource practices [in traditional societies] are ecologically driven and do not appear to correlate with attitudes (*including sacred prohibition*)."[33] There is no inevitable correlation between religion and ecological wisdom in particular: "Religious beliefs may well have the potential to be an important proximate cause of conservation—but the effectiveness of such prohibitions cannot be assumed."[34] Indeed, religion may well play in the opposite direction. Low herself cites the case of the Montagnai people of Canada, whose beliefs about beavers led them to adopt the practice of killing every beaver they encountered, useful or not. They feared that any surviving beaver would tell its kin that the Montagnai were hunting, thus making future hunts more difficult. Earlier we noted a similar belief and practice among the Plains Indians with respect to the buffalo. Shepard Krech III also writes about the Cherokee belief that if they failed to ask forgiveness of the deer they killed, then they would be punished with rheumatism. They *did* therefore need to approach and treat deer properly when they hunted them—at least in theory. But their beliefs did not prohibit them from killing *too many* deer. On the contrary, they believed that every deer killed before its allotted time was immediately resurrected and therefore that the supply of game could not be diminished through hunting. Such religious beliefs evidently contributed nothing to ecological wisdom.[35]

CONCLUSION
THE GOLDEN AGE THAT NEVER WAS

The story of the precivilizational golden age populated by indigenous people that is routinely articulated by the proponents of dark green religion is certainly somewhat more venerable than the story of the axial age. Its immediate origins are found in the early modern, rather than the late modern, period—the period in which the romantic movement first flourished, whose spirit is captured so well in William Wordsworth's "The Tables Turned":[36]

> One impulse from a vernal wood,
> May teach you more of man,
> Of moral evil and of good,
> Than all the sages can.

On this view, nature is a better and a purer teacher than civilization. Feeling is a more reliable instructor than intellect.

The story of a golden age populated by indigenous people is the more venerable story, but it is no less historically problematic than its axial age partner. The problem with romanticism, of course (for all its strengths), is that it is romantic, and not particularly clear headed on some matters about which it is important to be so. Romanticism does not necessarily represent things as they really are. This was Johann Wolfgang von Goethe's objection to the works of the romantic artist Caspar David Friedrich, of which he famously said (somewhat unfairly) that one might as well view them upside down.[37] Unfair or not, the question of reality is important. Are we really to believe, for example (as Wordsworth suggests), that one impulse from a vernal wood can teach us more about moral evil and good than all the thinkers through the ages who have reflected on the matter? I profoundly doubt it.

One of the questions that it is important to be clear headed about, of course, is this: What is really true about the past? It is just not true, it turns out, that there was, historically, the kind of golden age that dark green religion imagines. Even if we were to regard the lives of modern "primitive peoples," both in our immediate present and in the more recent documentable and recoverable past, as giving us reliable access to the distant past (and that is questionable)[38]—even so, those modern primitive lives would not provide us with a golden age. They would not, indeed, provide us with a *single* "original" age of *any* kind:

> There is no original human society, no basal human adaptation: studying modern hunter-gatherers in order to subtract the effects of contact with the world system (were that possible) and to uncover universal behaviors with the goal of reconstructing the original hunter-gatherer lifeway is simply not possible—because that lifeway never existed. We should accept it as highly possible, even likely, that modern diversity stems from original diversity in the foraging adaptations of behaviorally modern humans.[39]

This late modern assessment as to our modern inability to reconstruct "the state of nature" corresponds to Rousseau's early modern assessment of his own predecessors' inability to do so: "The philosophers who have examined the foundations of society have all felt it necessary to go back to the state of nature, but none of them has succeeded in getting there."[40] The dark green golden age of the Paleolithic period turns out to have been—to quote the anthropologist Thomas Headland and others—"the Golden Age that never was."[41] We should leave it in peace, in its (romantic) nonexistence.

7

You Can't Always Get What You Want
Desire (and Need) and the Past

Unless there is some kind of spiritual revolution that can keep
abreast of our technological genius, it is unlikely that we will save
our planet.

—Karen Armstrong, *The Great Transformation*

Why couldn't I—or any of my colleagues—see the magnitude and
the implications of the warfare that was displayed before our eyes
at El Morro? We were simply not conditioned to see it.
The idea that all was peaceful long before writing in the ancient
past was, and is, how most archaeologists and anthropologists
see the world.

—Steven LeBlanc, *Constant Battles*

I have no doubt that many readers will have found the contents of chapters 2, 3, 5, and 6 surprising—even shocking. The stories that we have
examined thus far in this book are widely believed to be true. It can
be disconcerting (to say the least) to discover just how little they are
based on evidence and how much evidence indeed stands against their
veracity. It *should* be disconcerting to find out (at least in the case of the
myth of the dark green golden age) how long this has been known by
serious scholars to be the case and yet how little impact this knowledge

83

appears to have had on believers. And this brings us to a puzzle. How is it that so many well-meaning people—indeed, so many smart, passionate, virtuous people—could have come to believe these two stories?

By way of getting to an answer to this question, let me recount an incident recalled by anthropologist Alice Ingerson from a course she once taught through Duke University's anthropology department:

> Many students enrolled in the course because they hoped to read about primitive or "first" peoples living "in harmony with nature." But when one student realized how difficult it was going to be to document any past harmony between culture and nature she broke into tears in my office, confessing that she didn't think she wanted to learn what she was going to learn in this class.[1]

Ingerson's story illustrates a perennial danger in human intellectual activity regarding the past. It is the danger that desire, and in fact need—more than evidence—will drive our reconstruction of the past. It is the danger that evidence itself will become unwelcome, insofar as it disturbs our settled understanding of the world. Desire and need will dominate the enquiry, and evidence may not seriously even be sought. Then, when evidence comes across our radar screens anyway, it will be ignored. It may even be repressed so that others cannot gain access to it. For we are committed to imagining the past that we desire, or need, in order to make sense of our lives and to provide ourselves with some underlying authority that might ground our present and future agendas. We are committed to the past as we *need* and *want* it to be; we are no longer interested in the past as it *was*.

The occasions, historically, upon which human beings and human societies have fallen prey to this temptation to draw the past only in a way that is convenient for their present, are too many to document here. The temptation is well understood by many and has often been written about and explored in art and literature, in both serious and not-so-serious ways. Among the not-so-serious contributions, for example, we might think of the film *The Planet of the Apes*, in which a central idea is that the governing apes know *something* about the true past of their planet. They refuse to recognize its significance, however, and they repress evidence relating to it; they are indeed prepared to go to great lengths to prevent the facts from coming out. The real past does not fit in with their present ideology. They desire, and they need, a different past.

It is only by factoring in desire and need, I think, that we can possibly solve the puzzle now under discussion. How is it that the two stories we have explored in chapters 1–6 are widely believed to be true, *even though* the evidence so strongly stands against their veracity? The answer, I believe, is that they *need* to be true if the past is to be useful to advocates in pursuit of a particular understanding of our present moment and a particular vision of the future. It is at least in part because each new story is perceived as meeting a pressing current need that each remains so popular and that there is apparently so little interest in many quarters in asking whether either is really true.[2]

The Need for an Axial Age

Why is the notion of an axial age so important to so many? What is at stake? We shall explore these questions by looking once again at three of the authors discussed in chapters 1 to 3.

Karl Jaspers

What was at stake for Karl Jaspers himself is already clear from the subtitle of his 1948 essay: "The Axial Age of Human History: *A Base for the Unity of Mankind*" (my emphasis). In a time of what the editor of the journal tells us were "exacerbated nationalisms," during which "the notion of the unity of mankind seems almost an anachronism," there was a tremendous need to regain such a base. Karl Jaspers, he goes on to tell us, "suggests that such a sense [of unity] is to be derived not from any single religious or philosophical system but from a specific historical experience, that of the Axial Age." The axial age provides a basis for the unity of humankind—and this is a pressing need. Jaspers himself later proposes that the axial age "helps us to overcome that narrowness which is the danger in every self-enclosed history," and draws us out to the boundless communication that is "the secret of achieving humanity, not in the prehistoric past but in ourselves." What is at stake for Jaspers is "nothing less than the question of how the unity of mankind can become concrete for each of us, of whatever tradition."[3]

The axial age, then, is important because it gives human beings something in common that might lead us to achieve humanity in the present, as we turn away from barbarism, nationalism, and the like. It is required as a substitute for the Christian or quasi-Christian ideas that predominated in the West in the preceding period from Augustine through to Hegel, in which the axis of history was understood (at least notionally) as the Christ event. This was something that Jaspers himself certainly did not believe. He regarded Jesus only as one of those historical figures "who confronts us . . . with the moral question of deciding for a life in the faith of God." The philosopher, he continues, "does not hear it in him alone, but also in the prophets of the Old Testament and in philosophers of high rank."[4] According to Voegelin, Jaspers was in fact disturbed by the language of orthodox Christian faith, precisely because he connected it with barbarism and fanaticism: "He sensed in it the transformation of existential truth into doctrine of which he recognized the murderous consequences in the practice of Communism and National Socialism."[5] So Jaspers needed a "big idea" with which to combat the prevailing idea of history, and he developed this idea in his myth of the axial age.

Ewert Cousins

When we turn to Ewert Cousins, writing around forty years later (1987), we find that his starting point lies in the need to explain the "global spirituality" that he alleges has arisen in the world in the course of those forty years. The axial age provides Cousins with his own explanatory key. It gives him an analogy in history to which he can appeal in order to ground his interpretation of his own present and his own predictions about the future. "The Axial Period," he tells us, "released a burst of spiritual energy whose influences are being felt even to this day." In what he suggests is currently a second axial period "we are caught up in a transformation of consciousness that is as momentous as that of the First Axial Period and that will have comparable far-reaching effects on religion and spirituality. . . . Whereas the First Axial Period produced individual consciousness, the Second Axial Period is producing global consciousness . . . in both a horizontal and a vertical sense." That is to say, human beings now think of themselves more and more *globally*. Second axial spirituality must also be global, both in the sense of advancing interreligious dialogue and empathy for the spirituality of others and in the sense of responding to "the prophetic call of the earth." The very future of the human race "will largely depend on the success of the world's religions to develop an adequate spirituality of the Second Axial Period."[6] For Cousins, then, the axial age plays a pivotal role in the story he wishes to tell about the spiritual progress of the human race. We are moving from one allegedly crucial period of enlightenment into what is alleged to be a second, and then we are moving into our future. Again we encounter a pressing need—the need to develop a particular form of globalized spirituality such that the human future will be secure.

Karen Armstrong

Karen Armstrong begins her *Great Transformation* with crisis: "Perhaps every generation believes that it has reached a turning point of history, but our problems seem particularly intractable and our future increasingly uncertain. Many of our difficulties mask a deeper spiritual crisis." Violence is a huge problem, and "we risk environmental catastrophe because we no longer see the earth as holy but regard it simply as a 'resource.'" Religion is no longer helpful, and people are turning to other things (e.g., art, sports, drugs) to give them a transcendent experience. We need a spiritual revolution, and in our time of need "we can find inspiration in the period that the German philosopher Karl Jaspers called the 'axial age' because it was so pivotal to the spiritual development of humanity." How so? She suggests that "we have never surpassed the insights of the Axial Age. In times of spiritual and social crisis, men and women have constantly turned back to this period for guidance." We ourselves need to recover the axial ethos—a spirituality of empathy and compassion, opposed to egotism and greed, violence and unkindness, directed toward the whole world, not just our own people. "In our global village, we can no longer afford a parochial or exclusive vision." Each generation has tried to adapt the insights of the axial sages to their own circumstances, and this must also be *our* task.[7]

As she concludes the book she returns to this same theme, in a chapter entitled "The Way Forward." At their core, she affirms, "the Axial faiths share an ideal of sympathy, respect, and universal concern." The axial sages were not much concerned with theological beliefs but with an alternative state of consciousness. We should follow their lead, looking for the "spiritual kernel" in religious doctrines (the "program for action" at their heart) and focusing on compassion while recoiling from violence. "Even though our problem is different from that of the Axial sages, they can still help us," for in various ways they were more advanced than we are.[8]

In Armstrong's thinking in *The Great Transformation*, then, the axial age functions as a gold standard in terms of our present and future actions. The prophets, mystics, philosophers, and poets of the axial age proclaimed an advanced and radical vision—so much so that "later generations tended to dilute it."[9] It is our task to recover it and to press on to fulfill it. The past is directly relevant to the matter of how we should view, and what we should do in, the present. This deep connection between the first and the current axial ages is also apparent in an interview that Armstrong gave to *EnlightenNext* magazine in 2005.[10] "All the great sages [of the axial age]," she reiterates, "were living in a time like our own—a time full of fear, violence, and horror. Their experience of utter impotence in a cruel world impelled them to seek the highest goals and an absolute reality in the depths of their beings." Today we are in the midst of a second axial age and "are undergoing a period of transition similar to that of the first Axial Age. . . . Once again, a radical change has become necessary."

In all of these authors, then—Jaspers, Cousins, and Armstrong— the axial age has an important role to play as they articulate their understanding of the present moment and their vision of the future. They *need* the axial age to ground the message they wish to proclaim about what we should believe and do now and as we move forward.

THE NEED FOR A DARK GREEN GOLDEN AGE

Again, why is the notion of a dark green golden age so important to so many—so important that the lack of evidence for its actual existence has also so routinely been ignored? What is at stake? The dark green golden age, it turns out, is *necessary*. It provides many people with legitimating authority for their agendas.

The darkness can sometimes be very dark indeed, not just in the sense of serious, but in the sense of sinister. Ter Ellingson quotes the nineteenth-century anthropologist Luke Burke (writing in 1848):

> The primitive races of mankind, while they continued pure, and in their native localities, were no more subjected to moral or physical evils than any other portions of the animal king-dom. . . . The period, therefore, of the isolation of the primitive races, was a golden age of peace, innocence, and happiness, in which physical evils were few and slight, and moral evils almost unknown.[11]

In this case, the myth of the golden age is deployed in support of a social vision centrally informed by notions of racial purity. It was while the primitive races remained "pure" that the golden age continued—a golden age not just of peace, innocence, and happiness but also of community of goods (i.e., holding resources in common). All races originally found themselves in circumstances exactly suited to their natures; that is why they flourished. We find ourselves now, unfortunately, in a different, mixed world, which is marked by physical and moral evil.

Mercifully this is not the kind of agenda that is being pursued by any of the thinkers I described in chapters 4 to 6. They do all have agendas, however, and I shall illustrate the point with reference to two authors whose work we discussed in those chapters.

Derrick Jensen

Derrick Jensen's social vision requires a dark green golden age for reasons very different to those of Luke Burke. Jensen dislikes civilization, not at all because there is a lack of racial purity within it, but because of its artificiality. It distorts reality; it overlays and represses what is natural. He anticipates a time in which all creatures will live within the world of natural cycles and will no longer be oppressed by notions of linear progress:

> People will live once again in the cycles of the earth, the cycles of the sun and the moon, the seasons. And longer cycles, too, of fish who slip into seas then return to rivers full of new life, of insects who sleep for years to awaken on hot summer afternoons, of martens who make massive migrations once every several human generations, of the rise and fall of populations of snowshoe hare and the lynx who eat them. And longer cycles still, the birth, growth, death, and decay of great trees, the swaying of rivers in their courses, the rise and fall of mountains. All these cycles, these circles great and small.[12]

He looks for an end to violence, against other human beings and against the natural world. He looks for an end to the hatred of life, the natural world, wild animals, women, children, and our embodiment.

But how is this social vision to be grounded? It must be grounded somewhere—somewhere other than in Jensen's own personal feelings about the civilized world. For Jensen does not want to say only that he *feels* a certain way. He wants to say that certain things are right (or natural) and that certain things are wrong (or unnatural). He also wants to propose that violence is an acceptable means to his ends, even though his ends include the end of violence.[13] His personal feelings are not sufficient to bear the weight of the great moral imperatives that he communicates to his readership, at the heart of which is the exhortation that we all need to participate in "taking down" civilization. However, he cannot appeal to any of the great world religions in order to ground his vision, for we recall that for Jensen these religions are part of the problem. They are transposable religions that do not emerge from the particularities of any landscape and that "lead people away from their intimate connection to the divinity in the land that is their home and toward the abstract principles of this distant religion."[14] So where can he turn?

As we know already, he turns to the distant, precivilizational past. There is such a thing as humanness, he says, and it is not compatible with civilization. To be human is to be precivilizational (or postcivilizational). People back then lived in exactly the way that Jensen is calling them to live in the future. They lived in harmony with the cycles of nature, with nature itself, and with each other. They lived peaceably in "relative equilibrium and sustainability," and they possessed leisure time, social equality, and food security. That is what it means to be human. Jensen then calls us to be human again, which sounds like something we would obviously want to be, as human beings. It also sounds like something for which it might be worth fighting—this prospect of throwing off the chains that enslave us, so that we can be what we were always meant to be. Indeed, we will be doing everyone else, and the planet, a great favor (Jensen suggests) if we accelerate the process by which civilization falls and humanness reasserts itself, since (we recall from chapter 4) "the longer we wait for civilization to crash . . . the worse things will be for those humans and nonhumans who live during it, and for those who come after."[15] Violence is justifiable, then, because (first) we are only claiming once again what has been taken away from us, because (second) we are assuring our long-term survival, and because (third) we are alleviating the suffering of those who come after us. We are possibly alleviating our own suffering as well, depending on how quickly civilization falls.

Jensen's vision of the *future* requires precisely the picture of the *past* that he paints. He needs the story of the dark green golden age to render his account of the future plausible and to lend authority to his advocacy of certain courses of action in the present. From the beginning we existed in a certain way, he suggests; that way of being was right and good, and we must now reclaim it.

David Suzuki

The story of the dark green golden age is just as wedded to a present agenda and a future vision in David Suzuki's case. He recognizes that for the planet to be saved, human beings need to develop a new sense of place in the world and a new reverence for nature. We need to reconceive of economics and politics as taking their lead from nature and functioning *in correspondence to*, rather than *dominating*, nature. We also need to reconceive of science and come to think of it in less reductionist ways. We need to become more human by learning to love other species and to live "in balance with the sacred elements." This significant change of perspective is necessary as a prerequisite to changes in behavior, such that we can achieve "sustainability within a generation."[16] But how is this change of perspective to be achieved? What is to be the foundation upon which Suzuki's vision of the future can be built?

Like Jensen, Suzuki wants to tell us more than just how he feels about the world. He wants to talk about right and wrong, good and bad. But, like Jensen, he cannot appeal to any of the world's great religions as the framework for his vision, since in his various writings he implicates these religions in the problem. Judaism, Christianity, Hinduism, and Islam have all abandoned any roots from which an appropriate vision might grow. Indeed, he closely associates the problematic scientific mind-set he is worried about with ancient Judeo-Christian (and Greek) thought. So where can he turn?

Like Jensen, he turns to the distant, precivilizational past—to what he calls the "historic precedent" among indigenous peoples of "sustaining a long-term ecological equilibrium with the natural world."[17] In this past human beings were at home. The wisdom of this past provides us with a map so that we too can find our way home. At some point we lost our way and forgot the narrative. We need to inhabit that narrative again. From the beginning we existed in a certain way; that way of being was right and good, and we must reclaim it. Suzuki needs this story. Without it he cannot address us effectively with his moral imperatives regarding how we must change.

Chief Seattle and His Friends

The depth of the need for the story of dark green religion that its proponents display, as well as the generally casual attitude toward evidence
that we encounter in their telling of it, is nicely illustrated by the now
well-known "Chief Seattle incident," recounted by Suzuki himself in
The Wisdom of the Elders. In 1854 a native leader, known to many modern people under the name Chief Seattle, allegedly delivered a speech
which has long been cited as "the single most eloquent, succinct, and
publicly accessible distillation of Native American nature-wisdom ever
published." However, it turns out that the genuine historical figure
behind this story was not named Seattle at all, and that although he
may well have given a speech back in 1854, many of the words attrib-
uted to him in modern versions of the speech most likely never came
out of his mouth. According to Rudolf Kaiser, who read a paper on this
topic to the European Association for American Studies in Rome in
1984, the speech "appears to be largely apocryphal."[18]

It did not, in fact, attract any real interest until the late 1960s and
early 1970s when it suddenly became significant for the environmental
movement. Here was a text that fitted beautifully with the preconcep-
tions of that movement—a text that was indeed "needed" in the context
of the environmental advocacy of that time. This, no doubt, explains
why no questions were apparently asked about its authenticity. It was
enthusiastically embraced as genuine, even though it should have been
obvious to the interested inquirer that the text of the speech varied significantly in different publications, which might have raised questions
about the nature of the original. But the speech was just too *useful*.
The evidence, including Kaiser's paper, was indeed largely ignored in
the years after 1984, and the Chief Seattle myth continued to prosper.
This was certainly still true in 1992, when Suzuki felt it necessary to
apologize to the readers of *The Wisdom of the Elders* for drawing attention to the problems with the speech—to readers who might "feel a
measure of betrayal and dismay upon learning the extent to which the
chief's original words have apparently been historically altered by out-
siders."[19] And, in spite of Suzuki's paragraphs on the subject, the Chief
Seattle myth remains still widely believed. Perhaps the truth remains
unwelcome.

It is, of course, commendable that Suzuki published his doubts
about the Chief Seattle speech. In this instance, at least, desire and
need did not trump evidence. One's enthusiasm for this development

is somewhat dampened, however, by what follows his exposé. What do we learn from the Chief Seattle case, in Suzuki's opinion? We learn that we must be careful to pay attention to such evidence as we possess about the provenance and the transmission of texts from the past. With respect to the native texts in which he is interested in *The Wisdom of the Elders*, Suzuki himself acknowledges that in general terms "it is probably impossible to be absolutely certain that any given Native narrative represents an 'authentic' Native voice without first documenting the text's entire convoluted history." And this is all well and good. The problem is that Suzuki then proceeds to present an entire book full of native narratives *without* "trying to confirm quickly and efficiently the accuracy of every [native] source we selected."[20] This *is* a problem, because the book is designed to communicate to its readers *ancient* native wisdom. The wisdom derives its authority precisely from its age. This being so, he cannot afford to be quite so relaxed about the provenance and the history of the transmission of his texts—granted the assumption that his readers are thoughtful people. He needs to demonstrate, in each case, that there is good reason to think that the text in question does, in fact, inform us about *ancient* native wisdom, rather than, for example, modern beliefs. But apparently, despite the cautionary tale of Chief Seattle, he does not consider this necessary. He needs the texts to be old and authentic, and so he simply asserts that they probably are.

There is a long history, in the telling of the story of the dark green golden age, of a similar carelessness toward evidence in pursuit of its telling—of desire and need dominating evidence. We see it in many of the accounts written by the Europeans who first traveled to and settled in North America, whose "arcadian and cornucopian images captured the imagination of contemporary readers, as they do today."[21] We see it, for example, in Lahontan's transformation (under the influence of Greek and Renaissance thought) of the Huron chief Kondiaronk into the native philosopher Adario, who bests him in debate.[22] We see it later, in the middle of the twentieth century (the period in which the Chief Seattle myth gains currency), as anthropologists popularize the idea "that prehistoric hunter-gatherer peoples were the most affluent humans who ever lived because they only had to work for 12 to 19 hours a week to feed themselves and their children on wild foods."[23] And we see it more recently in the work of someone like Derrick Jensen, who repeats various myths created prior to his time, including the "afflu-ence myth" just mentioned.[24]

The case is similar to that of the axial age. The dark green golden age has an important role to play in various authors' articulations of their understanding of the present moment and their vision of the future. They need this age in order to ground the message they wish to proclaim about what we should believe and do now.

CONCLUSION

The puzzle has been solved. It is at least in part because each of the stories about the world that we have been examining in chapters 1–6 is perceived as meeting a pressing need that each remains so popular—even though there is little to say in favor of the truth of either one. It is desire and need that explain how it is that so many well-meaning, smart, passionate, and virtuous people continue to believe them. They have become "conditioned" to believe them (to use Steven LeBlanc's word in the second epigraph to this chapter),[25] and they can no longer see the truth.

8

THE PAST RELOADED
A Brief History of Ancient Time

> ... without a factual understanding of what happened in the
> past we will never know where we have been or where we
> may be headed.
>
> —Charles Kay, afterword to *Wilderness and Political Ecology*

> In the application of Satyagraha, I discovered, in the earliest
> stages, that pursuit of truth did not admit of violence being
> inflicted on one's opponent, but that he must be weaned from
> error by patience and sympathy.
>
> —Mohandas Gandhi, quoted in R. K. Prabhu and U. R. Rao,
> *The Mind of Mahatma Gandhi*

If "the world that never was" has now been revealed in all its glorious
nonexistence, at least to the readers of this book, and the reasons so
many other people nevertheless fervently believe in it have been identified, the next question is: How *was* it, then? If the true story of the
past involves neither an axial age nor a preaxial golden age, what *does*
it involve? When the fog of myth disperses and we catch a glimpse of
what is really back there in ancient history before the common era—
when we gain the kind of "factual understanding" of it mentioned in
the Charles Kay quotation above—what do we see?

It is not my purpose in this chapter to provide an extensive account of ancient history. There are many, many, long books that have already provided us with such accounts, including the entire series of the Cambridge Ancient History. I am intent only on accomplishing two ends.

First, I shall lay out in a very general way the actual progress of ancient human history so far as we know it, from the beginning down to the period of Jaspers' axial age thinkers. I want to give the reader a sense of its actual shape once the distortions introduced by the notions of preaxial and axial have been removed.

Then second, and particularly, I want to spend some time describing in more detail the period within this history that has been mostly neglected to this point in the book. Inevitably, the myths that we have discussed so far have drawn our eye, on the one hand, to the precivilizational period of human history, and on the other hand to the period after the eighth century BCE. It is, however, important to grasp the true character of the intervening period, especially in view of the imprecise and sometimes downright misleading ways in which it has been treated in the discussions offered by the mythmakers. This is especially important if one is to understand properly the relationship of the axial age religions and philosophies to the intellectual and cultural environments out of which they emerged. I shall proceed in chapter 9 to consider one such tradition, the biblical tradition. Because that is where I am going, my description in the present chapter of the intervening period between the "golden age" and the "axial age" will focus particularly on the ancient Near East. However, I shall touch on other geographical areas as well.

In sum, the "brief history" provided in this chapter will focus on the rise of human civilization. I shall mention the *preceding* period only in passing. As to what *follows* the rise of human civilization, I shall essentially summarize and then expand upon the conclusions that should be drawn from my discussion in chapters 2 and 3.

RELIGION IN PREHISTORIC TIMES

I can be brief with respect to precivilizational human history not least because I do not need to repeat here my summary in chapter 5 of the little we know about the Paleolithic and Neolithic periods. Furthermore, many resources are available on the subject. I only wish to add the following, concerning what we do and do not know about *religion* in these periods.

We do have some evidence from Paleolithic and Neolithic times that is relevant to the question of religion. We encounter by way of archaeology, for example, the ancient habit of placing goods in graves, evidencing a belief in life after death.[1] There is some evidence, also, that certain animals may have been regarded as sacred. Ritual sites have been discovered, as well as sculpted figurines that may imply belief in a mother goddess. These are, however, meager findings. All sorts of speculation about the nature of early religion has arisen, then, on the basis of these meager findings and on the basis of dubious analogies drawn by modern people from modern hunter-gatherer societies—the kind of analogies that we have already discussed in chapter 5. If such analogies were to hold true, we might well imagine that prehistoric religion already involved the worship of many gods, albeit with one High God often presiding over the others. That is the picture that emerges from quantitative analysis of preindustrial traditional cultures of which we *do* know.[2] Whether such analogies really do hold true is, of course, in question. If we are not confident in them, then we must acknowledge that, overall, our understanding of the ancient condition of humanity remains *most* limited—including our understanding of its religion.

THE RISE OF COMPLEX SOCIETIES

Our understanding of the ancient past becomes less limited only as we begin to encounter the earliest of what anthropologists refer to as *complex societies*. That is to say, societies emerge in which we find cities containing thousands of people, rather than just villages containing a few hundred, and these people occupy specialized roles (e.g., fisherman, potter, priest) rather than simply being (all of them) farmers. They depend on other specialists, therefore, for their continued existence. In these societies we discover shared "national" religion rather than simply the religion of the family or village. We encounter pronounced social hierarchy, fixed from birth, from kings down to slaves, and rigorous obligations laid upon the lower classes with respect to the elites (e.g., paying taxes and fighting in wars).[3] These complex societies have left behind voluminous archaeological evidence in the form of residential and monumental architecture—the latter including pyramids, temples and palaces, and graves and their contents. Crucially, they have also left behind written texts.[4] We possess the words of these ancient peoples, which still communicate today, overtly or implicitly, what they thought, believed, and did. We are now for the first time in our human story on firmer ground in speaking about the reality of the distant past—precisely because we possess so many written texts that can be read alongside the archaeological evidence.[5] What is it exactly, then, that we know about this time?

The Gods of the Ancient Near East

As we enter the period of the Bronze Age civilizations that arise in the fourth millennium BCE in Mesopotamia and Egypt, we do see for certain (no matter what may be true about the preceding period) that religion in such complex societies *did* involve the worship of many gods, often with a High God presupposed in the background. In ancient Sumeria, for example, the sky god Anu played the role of the High God, begetting all the other gods but no longer playing an important role in everyday affairs. In his absence the storm god Enlil played the most important role, operating from his temple in the city of Nippur. But there were many other gods as well. There was Enki, god of the abyss, and Ninmah, the mother of the gods. There were gods of sun and moon, and of love, and of many other aspects of existence besides. In ancient Egypt we find a similar situation: a confusing array of gods and goddesses originating ultimately from an ancient progenitor or "One." The many arise from this "One."[6]

The gods were regarded throughout the ancient Near East as being themselves *part* of the cosmos, not as standing outside it. They came into being along with it, managing the cosmic system within parameters already woven into the very fabric of things which they themselves did not create and could certainly not ignore. They were viewed, indeed, very much as super–human beings—not dissimilar in many ways to the human beings with whom they shared the cosmos. They possessed "all the same qualities as humans . . . without as many limitations" (e.g., they were more powerful, without being omnipotent, and they lived longer). They were sexually active and they procreated; they made mistakes and committed crimes. They were not omniscient—they could experience uncertainty and confusion, and indeed "the whole range of human emotions," inclinations, desires, and needs.[7] They ate, slept, and had jobs to do. Yet they *were* gods, and human beings might easily get on their wrong side. The judgment of the gods could then fall upon them, even though they had not deliberately set out to offend. Therefore, the gods needed to be taken seriously.

The Importance of the Temple

The city-state had now become a standard form of social organization, and it was regarded "in Mesopotamia, and to a lesser extent in Egypt . . . [as] the ideal social context." Indeed, "the cosmos found its ultimate ordered state in the city." At the level of the city-state, taking the gods seriously required that temple rituals be continually observed by the priestly class created for that purpose. An ancient Near Eastern temple was primarily a palace for a god, and thus it was a place primarily for the performance of such rituals. It was not a place for what modern people might call worship, involving many ordinary adherents of a religion. It was thought to be the very center of the cosmos; "fertility, prosperity, peace and justice" emanated from the deity's presence there. It was "not only the cosmic center . . . [but also] the economic and moral center of the cosmos[,] . . . the ultimate focus of much of human activity." The governing idea was that a particular god had descended from the heavens to dwell in his or her temple. The major temple complexes in Mesopotamia indeed featured along with the temple a ziggurat—a tall tower indented with steps—so that the deity *could* descend from heaven to receive worship. The deity's presence in the temple was marked by an image or cult statue, in which the reality of the deity was embodied. Important rituals enabled this image to *function* as a god—mediating "worship from the people to the deity" as well as "revelation from the deity" back to the people (e.g., in court cases).[8] The gods had their needs met through the temple and its priests, and their image was resident in its midst; the people had their needs met by a contented deity.[9]

To ensure this contentment, in Mesopotamia the image of the god would be "awakened in the morning, washed, clothed, fed two sumptuous meals each day (while music was played in its presence), and put to bed at night."[10] It would be treated, in fact, in the way that a king should be treated. What was appropriate in such rituals was discerned in part intuitively and in part through specific commands given by the god and derived through divination. "When circumstances, omens, or prophetic oracles suggested that the deity was displeased, divinatory procedures would be initiated" to find out what to do, and then this solution would be added to tradition about what worked.[11] The gods were easily offended, experience showed; appeasement was therefore often necessary in order to protect both king and city. Given this reality, it can readily be understood that the Mesopotamian religious system was significantly marked by anxiety, especially since the gods might possess desires or needs that could only be guessed at. People could only hope that what they were doing was sufficient. The anxiety was less in Egypt only because the pharaoh was so closely identified with divinity (as we shall see in a moment) that people did not have to worry so much about what the gods were thinking. They already knew.

The Centrality of the King

Crucial to the society that was organized around the worship of the gods and the maintenance of their temples was the king. Kingship was regarded throughout the ancient Near East as a divine creation, given as a gift by the gods to human beings. Kings were regarded indeed as existing in closer proximity to the gods than any other mortal beings. They had been chosen by the gods and adopted as sons by them. The kings, for their own part, were eager to show that the gods supported their rule. The connection between the king and the gods was particularly strong in Egypt, where the monarch "was, on the whole, divinized to a higher degree than kings in the other cultures." He lived almost entirely in the realm of the gods. In Mesopotamia he usually only lived halfway, as it were, between the divine and human realms. But in both cultures it was the king above all who communed with the gods and mediated the power of the gods to his city and beyond. It was kings, more than anyone else, who were "expected to discern the divine will and facilitate its execution." In Egypt the strong identification of the pharaoh with deity led to robust confidence that the pharaoh's actions were, in fact, *the very acts* of a god. In Mesopotamia, with its somewhat lower view of kingship, more effort was given to *discovering* what the gods wanted and keeping the king *in touch with* deity. But the major responsibility of the king as a divine figure in both contexts "was to maintain order in the part of the cosmos that he could affect: his kingdom."[12]

Ordinary Religion

If the temple of the city-state was not a place for ordinary adherents of religion in the ancient Near East, how did ordinary religion work? For Mesopotamian people, "it was not considered obligatory for individuals to worship the state gods." Ordinary people tended rather to worship their family and ancestral gods, who would more likely be interested in them (and might perhaps advocate for them to the great gods). These were the "nearby" gods. They possessed a temple or shrine in the neighborhood, and people looked to them for the good things in life. But even though these gods were nearby, the same anxiety inevitably attended this kind of religion as attended state religion. "Inadvertent actions by the individual could suddenly draw the wrath of the deity," leaving worshippers vulnerable to negative forces because the god had withdrawn from them. The cause of the god's anger was usually unknown, so there was nothing specific that could be done to deal with it. Most people took refuge simply in general "acts of kindness and generosity"[13] toward the god, amidst frustration at not knowing for sure what the will of the god might be.

This was a world without clear revelation from the gods, and ancient Near Eastern prayers reflect it starkly. Sufferers might feel no guilt (not knowing how they had erred), yet they might experience shame because of society's rejection as a result of their misfortune. In such a context they ask in prayer for the god's favor to be restored and they expect that this will result in reintegration into society (shame removed and honor regained). Ancient Near Eastern wisdom literature also reflects this religious reality, when it addresses the matter of theodicy: why do people suffer even when they have pursued the will of the gods as best they know how? Sufferers would probably never know, because they lacked extensive and accurate knowledge as what pleased or offended deity. Divination might help, but that was a highly unreliable business, depending on fairly esoteric interpretive skills.[14]

Life after Death

What did people hope for, in terms of life beyond this life? Across the ancient Near East, we do find belief in an afterlife, variously expressed. In Egypt, from where most of our information derives, it could involve the judgment of the gods, leading to a nasty end if ethical and cultic behavior in life had not been well performed. Even in Egyptian texts, however, this is not commonly the case. More commonly the worst fate was regarded as becoming a homeless spirit, which might happen if a proper burial did not take place or funerary rites were not performed properly by surviving kin. Burial and mourning practices were, in fact, directed at making sure the ghost of a deceased person remained part of the community. The fundamental hope that people possessed was "that they would at the very least receive sustenance [from those who survived them] and that they would experience a peaceful rest [in the underworld] with a continuing sense of community with both ancestors and descendants who were still living."[15] Beyond that, they might hope that life would continue much as earthly life had been lived—especially if they were kings, for whom the experience of earthly life was relatively good. Kings might even hope for ascent into the heavens to be with the great gods.

It is understandable that people might hope for this last option particularly if they were Mesopotamians, because the underworld is not described in our ancient Mesopotamian sources as a particularly pleasant place. It is conceived of as a city ruled by the gods, especially by Queen Ereshkigal and her consort Nergal. To get to the city the dead person has to cross a demon-infested wilderness and then the river Hubur, then pass through seven walls and gates surrounding the city, before entering the city itself. The city was not believed, however, to be a happy destination at the end of this difficult journey. The dead lived there in poor conditions, which could be alleviated to some extent only by continued attention from those left behind. It was a rather gloomy prospect. In return for the attention paid to the dead, the living could hope to gain access to the future by way of necromancy.[16]

The Shape of Ancient Society

In the ancient world that I am describing, then, centrally important were the temples that housed the gods and the kings who were themselves always godlike and at best only semihuman. We may now add to the mix the important idea that the cities in which the kings ruled and in which the temple rituals were conducted were themselves regarded as primordial and built for the gods. They were not regarded as having been built primarily to accommodate human beings, any more than temples were considered to have been built, fundamentally, as worship places for human beings. All of this implies that human beings were not conceived of as having a very important place in the cosmos—a supposition that is confirmed, at least in the case of ancient Mesopotamia, by our Sumerian and Akkadian sources. These sources consistently portray human beings as having been created to labor for the gods—to do "work that is essential for the continuing existence of the gods . . . that they have tired of doing for themselves."[17] In other words, human beings represent slave labor, created as a cosmic afterthought to meet the needs of deity.

When we put together these two primary ideas—that human beings are an afterthought (just another part of the cosmos that helps the gods function) and that the king himself is a god, or very nearly a god—a particular view of early complex societies in the ancient Near East begins to emerge. These were societies designed to serve the needs of the gods, whose images were housed in their temples. But these were also societies designed to serve the human image of the gods that was the king. They were highly stratified, hierarchical societies—despotic societies. The exalted divinity of the Egyptian pharaoh implies a particularly extreme example of this manner of society in Egypt, although we have no Egyptian texts that offer explicit commentary on the purpose of the creation of humans.

They were stratified, hierarchical societies, and they were societies in which there was little inbuilt dynamic for change. The cosmos they reflected had been this way from the beginning and would continue to be this way in the future. Within the overall framework of serving the gods and the king, the aim of every family was simply to try to perpetuate itself as it moved *into* the future, since it was necessary to the dead that their descendants should not die out from the land of the living. Maintenance of order, of the status quo, was the concern at the family as well as at the city-state and ultimately the imperial level. Everything was structured to maintain that order, with its despot-king at its apex:

> Temple religions displayed all of the negative aspects of despotism, and for good reason. They were a leading institution of despotic states, so closely intertwined with political power that the two can be separated only crudely and with great analytic difficulty. That simple fact explains a great deal. From the perspective of the ruling elite in Sumer (throughout its many imperial manifestations), in Egypt, and in Mesoamerica, if to a lesser extent in Greece, the status quo could not be improved. So, nothing should be changed! And, at least in the religious sphere, for many centuries nothing was changed.[18]

Similar Societies beyond the Ancient Near East

All of this is what we see, in general terms (and allowing for variation), as we reach the Bronze Age in the ancient Near East and for the first time we can describe in more than vague outline what our human ancestors were thinking and doing.[19] We do not know much about what preceded these Bronze Age civilizations with their god-kings and their temple religions—about the period imagined into existence by the dark green religionists. However, we do know quite a bit about the ancient Near Eastern civilizations I have just been describing. We also know something about similar ancient civilizations that emerged subsequently in other parts of the world. We see such civilizations coming into existence in the Indus Valley around 2600–2000 BCE (the Harappan civilization, whose written language unfortunately remains undeciphered),[20] in China around 1800 BCE (the Shang civilization, which "marked the first widespread use of the distinctively Chinese forms of writing, architecture, art, and ideology"),[21] and in Greece.

Some of the similarities likely have nothing to do with direct influence, but others likely do. We know, for example, that although Greek city-states were in various important ways different from their ancient Near Eastern counterparts, nevertheless the influence of the ancient Near East upon Greece was initially significant. With respect to pre-Archaic art, "the gifts of the East to the Greek artist were manifold."[22] With respect to early Greek literature, like Homer's *Iliad* and *Odyssey* or Hesiod's *Theogony*, there is evidence of direct Eastern influence:

> Homer's decisive role in forming the world view of the Greeks
> for subsequent ages was achieved by the force of written culture
> into which the Greeks finally allowed themselves to be drawn
> right at this period. . . . [I]t is precisely the Homeric epoch of
> Greece that is the epoch of the orientalizing revolution. . . . The
> "miracle of Greece" is not merely the result of a unique talent.
> It also owes its existence to the simple phenomenon that the
> Greeks are the most easterly of the Westerners.[23]

Certainly with respect to religion, it is clear that the Greek gods display strong affinities with the ancient Near Eastern gods (although they were given different names). For example, like their ancient Near Eastern counterparts, they too were not regarded as the originators of law or ethics, which arose from within the human realm. They too were, in fact, subject to the greater principles of the cosmos (in this case fate, necessity, and justice), which they disregarded at their peril: "According to Herakleitos the sun remains within the bounds allotted to him, because otherwise the Furies, the servants of *dike* (justice), will find him."[24] The Greeks also believed in a rather unpleasant afterlife (at least for many people), like their ancient Mesopotamian counterparts. The religious similarities are so striking that Robert Parker can say straightforwardly: "Greek religion belongs to the class of ancient polytheisms: one can in very general terms compare the religions of Rome, of Egypt, of the ancient Indo-Iranians [i.e., the peoples who ultimately settled in what is now Iran, Pakistan, and India], and most of the religions of the ancient Near East."[25]

THE EMERGENCE OF THE AXIAL AGE RELIGIONS AND PHILOSOPHIES

It is against the background of these ancient civilizations, with their broad similarities as well their individual differences, that we then see emerging the various visions of the world that have been brought under the rubric of axial age religions and philosophies. As we discovered in chapters 2 and 3, however, when the fog of myth disperses and we catch a glimpse of what is really there, historically, it is in no way at all a distinctive axial age of the kind that its advocates propose.

What we see, instead, is certainly a remarkable period in human history, from the eighth to the second centuries BCE, when certain individuals or groups were to be found, in different places, setting their face against old ideas about the gods and against old understandings of world and society connected to these ideas. However, some of these people were simply following and developing a countercultural vision from an earlier time (e.g., the Israelites and the Zoroastrians). They were not initiating it. And crucially, the visions in question, both religions and philosophies, evidently differ from each other in their proposals about reality and how we should live in it. They do sometimes exhibit similarities, whether superficially or deeply. But often they are different from each other, and sometimes they are radically different. They also differ in how far they leave the old ways and ideas behind and how far they continue to make space for them.

In the end, it is just not possible to generalize, as Karl Jaspers and others have done, about an age in which there existed such different visions of reality as those represented by Confucius and Laozi in China; by the Upanishads and Buddha in India; by Zoroaster in Persia and the Hebrew prophets in Israel; and in Greece by Homer, Parmenides, Heraclitus, Plato, Thucydides, and Archimedes. Such generalization has only served to obscure the striking particularities of each vision. It has, indeed, done violence to these visions and their originators, as the mythmakers, in pursuit of their own truths, have essentially sought to suppress the voices from the past that contradict them. This is not only foolish but also wrong. "The pursuit of truth," as Gandhi rightly suggests, does not "admit of violence being inflicted on one's opponent." It is to this question of violence perpetrated against the individual traditions that we turn now in chapter 9.

9

ON LOVING YOUR DEAD NEIGHBOR
Violence, Knowledge, and History

What mattered was not what you believed but how you behaved.

—Karen Armstrong, *The Great Transformation*,
on the axial age

Has a nation changed its gods, even though they are no gods?
But my people have changed their glory for something that
does not profit.

—Jeremiah, inhabitant of the "axial age"

The story about our ancient human past that I have just recounted is, I believe, true. Although it is brief, it is consistent with the evidence. Specifically, it is true (albeit brief) in its presentation of ancient religion and philosophy. It attends to what can and cannot be known about ancient religions and philosophies, it attends to their particulars where they *can* be known, and it avoids generalizing in such a way as to obscure these particulars. It not only honors the past, it honors the religions and philosophies of the past. It does them no violence. It seems to me that such avoidance of violence matters. We ought, I think, to try to treat our neighbors in the past just as well as we try to treat them in the present. We ought not to misrepresent them, we ought to try to understand what they mean and not twist their words, and we ought not simply to use them in pursuit of our own agendas. These are ethical imperatives that many people try to live by in the present. I do not see why they should not apply to the past as well.

It is my contention that the mythmakers discussed in chapters 1–6, even though they share a serious commitment to nonviolence in the present and the future, have *failed* to avoid inflicting violence upon the religions and philosophies of the past. I do not suggest that they necessarily intend to be violent, or that they themselves understand what they are doing as violent. Nevertheless, violence occurs. They tell us what they would *like* ancient philosophies and religions to have said about the world, rather than what they did say (and in some cases still do say). They see what is not there, and they ignore what *is* there. There is a studied disregard for particular, annoying facts, which are routinely stripped out of these ancient religions and philosophies in pursuit of what they allegedly have in common. Generalizations (sometimes wild) are advanced, and serious misrepresentation occurs.

The case study I want to use to illustrate this violence is biblical, specifically Old Testament religion. This is my area of professional expertise, and it is also my own still-living tradition, in the sense that Christians share the Old Testament as Scripture with Jews (who refer to it as Tanakh). I can well imagine that there may be other readers of this book who will have their own issues with the mythmakers—who will feel aggrieved about how their own ancient, but still living, tradition has suffered at their hands. I hazard a guess that these will include readers who feel offended at how reduced and impoverished a vision emerges from this mythmaking of significant worldviews such as Hinduism, Buddhism, or Confucianism. However, I need at this point to leave these many people to articulate their own perspectives on the matter. I have my own particular concern: that it is certainly the case that the Old Testament literature has been grievously misrepresented in the midst of all this mythmaking. It is certainly the case that violence has been done, however unintentionally, to this "old story," the biblical story, which the mythmakers have been concerned above all others to replace with their own "new stories" because of its historical importance in Western societies.

Karen Armstrong (Again)

We see the violence to which I am referring, by way of a first example, in Karen Armstrong. In chapter 3 we noted her curious reading (in her *Short History of Myth*) of the biblical book of Genesis, in which Genesis is read, quite against the grain, as presenting the rise of civilization as a disaster. We noted also her misleading inclusion of the biblical prophets within the group of axial age sages who taught their disciples to look within themselves for truth. The misrepresentation continues on the immediately following pages of the same book, where Armstrong contrasts the picture of God painted in the story of Abraham, where God eats and converses with Abraham, with the God of the later prophets, who are alleged to have found "the supreme reality . . . impossibly difficult to access."[1] One might well wonder, then, why it is that we find the prophet Jeremiah so regularly proclaiming to his audiences that he knows what God's word is for them—indeed, why it is that true prophets are distinguished from false ones precisely in that the former have access to the very council of God, and the latter do not:

> Do not listen to the words of the prophets who prophesy to you; they are deluding you. They speak visions of their own minds, not from the mouth of the LORD. . . . For who has stood in the council of the LORD so as to see and to hear his word? Who has given heed to his word so as to proclaim it? . . . I did not send the prophets, yet they ran; I did not speak to them, yet they prophesied. But if they had stood in my council, then they would have proclaimed my words to my people. (Jer 23:16-22)

One might well wonder, also, why so much of the book of Jeremiah consists of prophetic prayers of a highly engaged and passionate nature, directed to a highly personal God. It is simply foolish to speak (as Armstrong does) of this biblical, prophetic outlook as if it were in any significant way similar to that of Confucius, who "believed that the Dao, the supreme reality, was now so alien from the world of men that it was better not to speak about it."[2] It is equally foolish to set up a false contrast between the God of Abraham and the God of the later biblical prophets.

Jeremiah also shows up in *The Great Transformation*, where early on he is mentioned as one who lived in the axial age with its common vision of the world. One of the many problematic statements about the axial age in these opening pages is partially reproduced in the first epigraph to this chapter: "What mattered was not what you believed but how you behaved. Religion was about doing things that changed you at a profound level . . . religion *was* compassion."[3] Jeremiah would no doubt have been interested in this description of what "mattered" in the time in which he allegedly lived. For the fact is that when Jeremiah is called by God to be a prophet, the message he is given to proclaim is that God's judgments are going to fall on people precisely "for all their wickedness in forsaking me; they have made offerings to other gods, and worshiped the works of their own hands" (Jeremiah 1:16). What they believe about God, and about God's relationship to other entities regarded as gods, appears to matter greatly in this passage. Then in Jeremiah 2:5-11 we read the following:

> Thus says the LORD:
> What wrong did your ancestors find in me that they went far
>   from me,
> and went after worthless things, and became worthless
>   themselves?
> They did not say, "Where is the LORD who brought us up from
>   the land of Egypt,
> who led us in the wilderness, in a land of deserts and pits,
> in a land of drought and deep darkness,
> in a land that no one passes through, where no one lives?"
> I brought you into a plentiful land to eat its fruits and its good
>   things.
> But when you entered you defiled my land, and made my
>   heritage an abomination.
> The priests did not say, "Where is the LORD?"
> Those who handle the law did not know me;
> the rulers transgressed against me;
> the prophets prophesied by Baal,
> and went after things that do not profit.
> Therefore once more I accuse you, says the LORD, . . .
> Has a nation changed its gods, even though they are no gods?
> But my people have changed their glory for something that
>   does not profit.

Belief *matters* in the book of Jeremiah. It is intrinsically related to practice. In Jeremiah these are two sides of the same coin—as they are for
all the biblical prophets. The idea that they thought that "what mattered was not what you believed but how you behaved" is ridiculous.
And Armstrong's attempt to present Jeremiah in particular as the pre-
dictor and facilitator of Israel's transition into a more enlightened state,
in which external religion gave way to a discovery of "the more interior
and direct knowledge of the Axial Age," is profoundly unconvincing.[4]
This is not the figure of Jeremiah who emerges from a reading of the
actual book of Jeremiah.

The biblical story does not fare well in Karen's Armstrong's writings. Violence is done to it. It is not done just to Jeremiah, but also to
other "neighbors of the past" like Job. One would have thought, frankly,
that poor old Job had suffered enough already. But his voice is arguably more effectively suppressed by Armstrong's book than by the three
friends who gather to "comfort" him in his *own* book.

LYNN WHITE

The biblical story fares no better in the literature emerging out of
dark green religion. I shall focus on three examples, albeit not at equal
length. Highly influential here, even though its central arguments
have been heavily critiqued, is an essay written by Lynn White in 1967
(delivered in 1966 in oral form) on the historical roots of our present
ecological crisis.[5] Claiming to describe what it is that Christianity has
told people historically about their relations with their environment,
White writes:

> By gradual stages a loving and all-powerful God had created
> light and darkness, the heavenly bodies, the earth and all its
> plants, animals, birds and fishes. Finally, God had created Adam
> and, as an afterthought, Eve to keep man from being lonely.
> Man named all the animals, thus establishing his dominance
> over them. God planned all of this explicitly for man's benefit
> and rule: no item in the physical creation had any purpose save
> to serve man's purposes. And, although man's body is made of
> clay, he is not simply part of nature: he is made in God's image.
> Especially in its Western form, Christianity is the most anthro-
> pocentric religion the world has seen.[6]

I do not dispute that there are Christians who hold more or less the view of the world that White outlines here, and who, as a result, have come to hold a quite instrumentalist and pragmatic view of the rest of creation in relation to themselves. But if he seriously thinks that he is describing what the Hebrew texts in the Bible have to say about such matters, White is badly mistaken.

There is, first, no biblical warrant for the idea that "no item in the physical creation had any purpose save to serve man's purposes." On the contrary, created beings each have their own purpose and destiny under God, independent of their relationships with human beings. Psalm 104:10-23 beautifully reminds us of this, as the following abbreviated version of it reveals:

> You make springs gush forth in the valleys; they flow between
>   the hills,
> giving drink to every wild animal; the wild asses quench their
>   thirst.
> By the streams the birds of the air have their habitation;
> they sing among the branches. . . .
> You cause the grass to grow for the cattle, and plants for
>   people to use,
> to bring forth food from the earth, and wine to gladden the
>   human heart,
> oil to make the face shine, and bread to strengthen the human
>   heart.
> The trees of the LORD are watered abundantly,
> the cedars of Lebanon that he planted. . . .
> The young lions roar for their prey, seeking their food from
>   God.
> When the sun rises, they withdraw and lie down in their dens.
> People go out to their work and to their labor until the
>   evening.

There is no basis here for any "axiom that nature has no reason for existence save to serve man."[7]

Nor is it the case that "God planned all of this [creation] explicitly for man's benefit and rule." White's error here is related to two subsidiary errors. He imagines, first, that the naming of the animals in Genesis 2 is about establishing dominance over them, but this is not the case. Throughout the ancient Near East naming was part of the process by which something came into existence. Naming went along with assigning a function to an entity. Thus an Egyptian text, the *Ritual of Amun*, tells us that prior to creation "no god had come into being and no name had been invented for anything." The Mesopotamian text *Enuma Elish* likewise speaks of the period when "no gods were manifest, nor names pronounced, nor destinies decreed."[8] The birth of the gods is intrinsically bound up with the assigning of their functions and roles in the cosmos; more generally, to create something is to name it and give it a function within an ordered world.

With this background in mind we quickly understand that, in naming the creatures in Genesis 2, the human being is joining with God in creating the world, not least by assigning the animals *roles* in the world. Naming is not about dominance but about where all of God's creatures fit in the cosmos (as described in Psalm 104). More generally, although naming is indeed often carried out in the Old Testament by those who have authority over others (e.g., parents), it cannot be demonstrated that the act of naming in itself *involves* the assertion of authority or dominance. A strong example that points in the opposite direction is Hagar's naming of God in Genesis 16:13.

The second subsidiary error is that White believes that, in the biblical worldview, our human status as creatures made in God's image results in our not being truly *part* of nature but somehow transcendent over it. This is not true either. In Genesis, it is as resolutely mortal, creation-bound persons that human beings are *also* God's image bearers. It is true that in biblical thinking this involves (in Gen 1) "ruling" over creation—that the metaphor of kingship is deployed by the biblical authors to describe the human vocation as kingly. But in the context of the ancient world out of which our biblical texts emerged, the king did not only *rule* but was also tasked with *looking after the welfare* of his subjects and ensuring justice for all (see, e.g., Psalm 72). In biblical thinking, he did this under God, who is alone truly King and to whom the whole earth belongs and everything in it (Psalm 24:1). Genesis 2 makes it clear what this actually looks like in relation to the rest of creation, when it exegetes the "ruling" of Genesis 1 in terms of earth keeping:

> The LORD God took the man and put him in the garden of Eden
> to till it and keep it. And the LORD God commanded the man,

"You may freely eat of every tree of the garden; but of the tree of
the knowledge of good and evil you shall not eat, for in the day
that you eat of it you shall die." (Gen 2:15-17)

Here the world is portrayed as a garden, in which human beings live
in harmony with their kin (the animals) and with God, and the human
vocation is described in the language of priesthood. Human beings are
"to till it [the garden] and keep it." More literally, they are "to serve
it [Heb. 'abad] and keep it [Heb. shamar]." This is the very language
that is used in Numbers 3:7-8 of the tasks of the priests in the move-
able temple known as the tabernacle. The priests there are supposed
to "perform [shamar] duties . . . doing service ['abad] at the tabernacle;
they shall be in charge of [shamar] all the furnishings of the tent of
meeting, and attend to the duties for the Israelites as they do service
['abad] at the tabernacle." In the biblical perspective, then, the work of
the human being in God's world is religious work. We are to look after
sacred space—the dwelling place of God—on behalf of the one who
created it. Creation is absolutely not designed "explicitly for man's benefit" in our biblical tradition. Human rule is, in fact, designed for the
benefit of all creation.

Lynn White has done violence to the Old Testament literature. I am
sure that he did not intend to do such violence, but he accomplishes it
nonetheless. He misrepresents what it is saying.

Evelyn Stokes

Although there is very little to be said for arguments of the kind that
White advances here, these are nevertheless arguments that appear
or are alluded to with wearying frequency in the literature of the dark
green religionists, along with other arguments of his which are similarly
problematic.[9] In fact, they are not often repeated even as *arguments*,
but simply as self-evident truths. They form part of a dark green faith
tradition about the old story—a (new) tradition about this story that
apparently everyone just knows to be true, even though few can possibly
have bothered to read the primary biblical literature that is supposed to
articulate this supposedly biblical view. So it is that Evelyn Stokes, for
example, in the course of a description of the Māori relationship with
the land in New Zealand, can offer us these ill-considered comments:

> Māori saw themselves as part of their environment, at one with
> it, not dominating it. This relationship was an intensely practi-
> cal one of using the resources of land and sea for daily suste-
> nance, but was also deeply spiritual, involving recognition and
> propitiation of ancestor gods. Such ideas do not always sit easily
> with Pākehā [i.e., non-Māori New Zealanders], accustomed to
> individual property rights and concepts derived from Judaeo-
> Christian tradition, and the divine command to Adam and Eve,
> "Go out and subdue the earth."[10]

She goes on to cite with approval a report of the Waitangi Tribunal that
was set up in New Zealand in 1975 to deal with land claims: "Māori saw
themselves as users of the land rather than its owners." Her assumption is clearly that the Māori way of looking at such matters is entirely
different from the biblical way. Yet not only do Genesis 2 and Psalm
24:1 oblige us to set the Genesis command to "subdue" in the context
of everything else God is doing in the world, but Leviticus 25:23 explicitly says, "the land shall not be sold in perpetuity, for the land is mine
[God's]; with me you are but aliens and tenants." The Israelites are *not*
to regard the land as *theirs*. This is quite clear—*if* one reads the biblical text. The land is given to the Israelites as a gift by God, just as the
whole earth is given as a gift to all of God's creatures. Biblically, it is a
grave mistake to think about it in any other way (Deuteronomy 9:4-6;
26:9, "He brought us into this place and gave us this land"). It is God's
garden; we are merely the gardeners.

Derrick Jensen (Again)

Finally, among our examples from dark green religion, we may note a
number of comments from Derrick Jensen. Like Lynn White, Jensen
regards the Genesis command about being fruitful, multiplying, and
exercising dominion over other creatures as problematic. He thinks of
it as informing those who "define *success* not as living in place over
time but as conquering all other cultures and conquering the planet."
He implicates the same text elsewhere in creating one of the central
myths of American culture: "the desirability of growth, a parasitic
expansion to fill and consume its host."[11] Like White, he fails to read
the biblical text in its biblical context.

Going beyond White, Jensen implicates biblical notions about the
jealousy of God in producing the hegemony of the gods of modern

science, capitalism, and civilization. He does so without taking so much as a moment to ponder the meaning of the word *jealousy* when predicated of God, while apparently remaining unaware of the irony of blaming biblical injunctions against idolatry for producing idolatry.[12] Jealousy is in essence an intolerance of rivals, and God is indeed often said in the Old Testament to be intolerant in just such a way of other gods. For example, "you shall not make for yourself an idol, whether in the form of anything that is in heaven above, or that is on the earth beneath, or that is in the water under the earth. You shall not bow down to them or worship them; for I the LORD your God am a jealous God" (Exodus 20:4-5). From a biblical perspective this jealousy is only right—there is, after all, only one God—but also good news for his human creatures, for it is jealousy that leads God to campaign against the false gods who can do human beings no good at all even if they should devote themselves to them. From a biblical perspective this would *include* the gods of modern science, capitalism, and civilization. To blame such ancient monotheism for modern idolatry is very strange. In biblical thinking it is precisely the jealousy of the one God that provides the greatest hope that the weak and oppressed of the earth can be released from the grip of the wicked and their false gods. Psalm 94:1-3 cries out for this justice:

> O LORD, you God of vengeance,
>   you God of vengeance, shine forth.
> Rise up, O judge of the earth;
>   give to the proud what they deserve!
> O LORD, how long shall the wicked,
>   how long shall the wicked exult?

Finally, Jensen characterizes Christian faith as "perceiving the world . . . as an evil place, a vale of tears where the enemy death constantly stalks, a place that is not and can never be as real as the heaven where bodies—these wild and incontrollable *things* we've come to see as so flawed—no longer exist, a place that can never be home."[13] I do not doubt that Jensen has met some people claiming to be Christians who hold more or less this view of things, but if he has, then these are people who are also (like Jensen) not actually reading biblical texts. The *texts* (like Psalm 104) constantly rejoice in God's creation. They take material existence deeply seriously, and they marvel in particular at how we human (embodied) beings are "fearfully and wonderfully made"

(Psalm 139:13-16). This is world-affirming, matter-affirming literature. The world is not divine, certainly, and it is not to be worshipped. But this does not imply a devaluing of creation. It is to be well looked after (by "gardeners," as we have seen) simply *because* it is a creation—the temple-cosmos of the Creator God, filled with the creatures that he has made. God also lives here, transcendent over creation but also immanent within it. And as a sacred place in which God himself dwells, the world is (as it is, and not in some other form) a fundamentally *good* place. Genesis 1 constantly reminds us of this, in verses 10, 12, 18, 21, and 25. It is a place where God's blessing is experienced by his creatures (Genesis 1:22 and 28). It is a place of order and beauty as well as of the provision of material needs: the trees in the garden are said to be "pleasant to the sight *and* good for food" (Genesis 2:9). It is a place under God's ongoing, active care:

> You visit the earth and water it,
> you greatly enrich it;
> the river of God is full of water;
> you provide the people with grain,
> for so you have prepared it.
> You water its furrows abundantly,
> settling its ridges,
> softening it with showers,
> and blessing its growth . . .
> the meadows clothe themselves with flocks,
> the valleys deck themselves with grain,
> they shout and sing together for joy. (Ps 65:9-13)

The world that is created by God is, in biblical thinking, *good*. It is not, as Jensen claims, "an evil place," although there is evil in it, and there may be tears shed in it, and of course there *is* death in it. But it is a good place, and it *is* "home." There are problems that arise *within* the world, certainly, which need to be overcome. The world itself is, however, not a problem to be overcome.

There *are*, of course, religions and philosophies in which the world *is* a problem to be overcome. We find such a view of the world in various religious traditions of the East, for example, which tend to share the common ancient Near Eastern view that reality is ultimately impersonal and therefore that our own human (and indeed *embodied*)

personhood is problematic. The transient phenomena of historical, personal existence are not of ultimate importance, on this view.
Indeed, they obscure the truth about our destiny, which we can only
begin to fulfill by withdrawing from attachment to the world as we
find it. Such a view is found, for example, in both Hinduism and Buddhism. Here the world as we know it through our senses *is indeed* an
obstacle to the attainment of some greater good for which we should
be striving. Here indeed this world "can never be as real as the heaven
where bodies . . . no longer exist."[14]

This same basically suspicious and negative attitude toward the
world as we know it also shows up in different forms in the philosophy
and religion of the West. The ancient Pythagoreans shared with Eastern thinkers a belief in the "wheel of existence" which involves multiple
reincarnations until we gain "release" from the world. They embraced
specifically those strands within Eastern thinking in which was imagined an essential human self or immortal soul.[15] For Plato, too, there
existed elsewhere a "real," eternal, unchanging world, immeasurably
superior to the world of our experience, to which human beings currently have only intellectual access. All human souls, Plato posited,
lived at one time in this higher world, before the union of each immortal soul with a body. Philosophy, for Plato, consisted in the effort to
rise through pure thought from the knowledge of the appearance of
things to the knowledge of the reality itself. We thus propel ourselves
along a path that in the end, when reincarnations have ceased, will
lead to the release of our immortal soul from its entrapment in the
changing world.[16] The problematic nature of the world with respect
to our human destiny is also an important tenet of the various forms
of Gnosticism that arose in the Greek and then Roman Empires after
Plato's time and of the Manichaeanism that arose in the third-century
CE Persian Empire. Both Gnosticism and Manichaeanism regarded
matter itself as evil.[17]

Biblical faith has often been associated, historically, with such negative or suspicious attitudes toward the world as we find it. Jensen is not
the first to do so. To read the biblical literature in such a way is, however, to do it violence. In biblical thinking, the world is categorically not
a problem to be overcome. It is not a mistake. It does not trap human
beings in a place where they were never meant to be and in which they
do not truly belong. It is not a place of shadows and illusions that only

dimly, if at all, reflect a "real" world that exists somewhere else. It does not lack something in being experienced in personal terms by human beings, while reality is allegedly impersonal. Its physical, sensual pleasures are not traps set to ensnare the soul. On the contrary, the world is a wonderful place, created in such a way as to be exactly the right place—a good and a beautiful place—for the flourishing of the creatures, personal and otherwise, of the one God who is personal. The following description of the Jewish perspective on life in creation captures this well: "Since God created all things good, humans have the obligation to enjoy and enhance life. Good food, wealth, and sexual pleasure are all gifts of God, and should be enjoyed in the rightful way."[18] Any good gift of God can of course be abused and take human beings off track. That is well understood in the biblical tradition, as it is in all the Abrahamic faiths. But the world that God has made is not intrinsically problematic in any way with respect to human destiny.

CONCLUSION

The old story told in the biblical literature has not been treated well by the mythmakers, who have sought to replace it with their own. Indeed, the level of mistreatment, historically, is such that this old story is apparently no longer known, even in its outline form, by many of those who now so quickly dismiss it. It is certainly not known in its many *particulars*. Violence has led, as it so often does—and whether or not it is understood as violence by its perpetrators—to a silencing of story. It has led to an absence of knowledge. I refer readers who would like to take further steps to remedy this deficit to a larger book of mine, which retells the old, biblical story at much greater length: *Seriously Dangerous Religion: What the Old Testament Really Says and Why It Matters.*[19]

ON TRUTH AND CONSEQUENCES
Why Myths about the Past Matter

Romantic misconceptions might not matter, except that the
conventional wisdoms arising from them generate normative prescriptions. . . . Current strategies of environmental and conservation education reflect our faith in such ideals . . . but typically
without tests of whether any of the assumptions are true.

—Bobbi Low, "Behavioral Ecology of Conservation
in Traditional Societies"

If we really want to restore Yellowstone's preeminent predator,
then the public should be lobbying for the return of the park
to Native Americans.

—Charles Kay, afterword to *Wilderness
and Political Ecology*

The mythmakers behind the myths of the axial age and the dark green
golden age do violence to the ancient religions and philosophies they
claim to describe. They do so in the course of distorting the past in
general. This is problematic in terms of ethics. It *matters*, because it is
morally wrong. We should not disrespect the past or the peoples of the
past. We have a duty to tell the truth.

Do the distortions matter for any other reason? I believe that they do. They matter because the past, the present, and the future are so closely bound up with each other. As the philosopher Alasdair MacIntyre suggests, the story in which I believe myself to be a character is also the story in which I come to understand my nature and my destiny.[1] My sense of who I am, where I should be heading, and what I should do next—I "own" all these in the context of what I believe to be true about the world, its history and destiny, the nature of divinity and humanity, and the good society. It is all very much bound up with the story in which I believe I find myself.

This includes the parts of the story that are now in the past. If I do not get the story straight with respect to the past—if I start believing claims about the past that are simply not true—then there is a very good chance that I will make significant mistakes in my thinking and living in the present. There is also a very good chance that I will go astray in my planning and advocacy with regard to the future. This is the reality that Charles Kay has in mind in the first epigraph to chapter 8: "Without a factual understanding of what happened in the past we will never know where we have been or where we may be headed."[2] If, in fact, there was an axial age—if there was before that a Paleolithic golden age—then these ages may indeed offer us insights that will help us in our present moment of need. If these are fantasies, however, then their relevance to our present moment becomes less clear. Indeed, allowing a fictional past to dictate our approach to the present and to the future may well be very damaging and dangerous—as the epigraph from Bobbi Low at the head of *this* chapter suggests. Even while possessing the best of *intentions* in terms of looking after our fellow human beings, other creatures, and the planet itself, we may go badly wrong in our *practice*, because we begin in the wrong place. We may indeed end up harming the very people—the very world—that we are intent on trying to save.

In this final chapter, I simply wish to illustrate the danger briefly with respect to two issues, before bringing my whole argument to a conclusion. The first is the issue of the human rights of native populations in Latin America. The second is the issue of wilderness care in the United States. In both cases, it is clear that the way we imagine the past can have significant implications for the ways we act in the present and plan for the future.

Noble Savages and Human Rights

Consider, first, the impact of what others have called the myth of the ecologically noble savage on the lives of those modern "primitive peoples" who are widely regarded by the proponents of dark green religion as preserving ancient ecological wisdom. Consider what has happened to *them* because others have regarded them (wrongly, as it turns out) as inheriting a long tradition of living in harmony with nature—taking care neither to exceed in population the carrying capacity of their environment nor to damage the earth or its various animal populations.

Allyn Stearman notes how negative the consequences can in fact be for native peoples who are first believed to be ecologically noble savages and then subsequently discovered not to be so at all. She describes how the Yuquí of eastern Bolivia were first granted land rights by the Bolivian government, only to have them later threatened. They were threatened in part because of "an increasing awareness that these indigenous peoples do not fit the widely publicized image of Indians as conservationists." She further describes how the decision of the Brazilian Kayapó to begin exploiting their natural resources "has fueled a growing movement in the Brazilian Congress to reduce Indian lands and make it more difficult to legalize indigenous territories." She continues, "One cannot but wonder if this reaction would have had the same repercussions if the Kayapó had not received international attention as 'natural conservationists' and 'keepers of the forest.'"[3]

The reaction is not just from politicians. Alice Ingerson quotes one environmentalist speaker at a conference as follows: "If we can't count on culture to make indigenous peoples conserve the rain forests, then turning the forests over to them would be like turning the forests over to the random assortment of people you saw in the airport on your way to this meeting." She cites the example to illustrate the long-term problem of anthropologists using "ahistorical romanticism as a way of encouraging environmentalists to see forest peoples as 'adapted to' or 'defenders of' supposedly stable ecosystems."[4] In the end, the rights of these peoples suffer. A myth about the *past* leads on to a negation of their rights in the *present*. Myths (apparently) matter.

Flora Lu Holt discusses how this reality has affected the Huaorani Indians of Ecuador, who, like many indigenous populations in Amazonia, are experiencing population growth as a result of abandoning warfare and infanticide and of the introduction of modern medicine.

They have adopted new technologies and are increasingly involved in the market. At the same time, their previous beliefs about natural plenty are changing, and awareness of the need for conservation is emerging—something that *can* emerge only when there is "stress on the resource base, made tangible through scarcity and/or increases in work effort, with significant repercussions for the user group." Ironically, it is precisely as this conservation awareness is *emerging* that the Huaorani and peoples like them have come to be regarded by some outsider conservation biologists and ecologists as "enemies of nature who have lost their 'pristine' and 'traditional' ways."[5]

They are perceived in this way because their populations are growing and they possess new technologies as well as new market incentives. What is really just an adaptation of "their economic activities and technologies for survival in changing circumstances . . . is taken as evidence that they have lost their 'natural conservationist' tendencies." This can lead to outsider advocacy of "draconian measures to exclude locals, both in terms of a place at the decision-making table and an ability to inhabit areas deemed ecologically fragile."[6] But these peoples did not, of course, have any "*natural* conservationist tendencies" to begin with, for "'conservation' is not a state of being. It is a response to people's perceptions about the state of their environment and its resources, and a willingness to modify their behaviors to adjust to new realities."[7]

THE GARDEN OF EDEN AND WILDERNESS POLICY

Consider, second, the impact on modern wilderness policy of the idea that there was a time when human populations lived in harmony with a pristine natural environment. Gerald Williams notes the impact, for example, of the denial of the extent to which Native Americans shaped their environment through fire. This is connected to the romantic view of pre-European North America that we discussed in chapter 6, according to which these natives simply lived in harmony with their environment rather than significantly impacting it. Williams notes that this denial has produced historically in the United States an approach to the conservation of forests in which fire has been anathema. Yet "the basis for much of the 'forest health crisis' of today really started with the almost complete cession of Indian burning during the early 1700s in the East and the 1850s in the West. It is no wonder that ecosystems today have daunting forest health problems (accumulate fuels, diseases, and insects)."[8] The myth of the pristine wilderness has shaped public policy in the United States to the detriment of the health of the forests, which *requires* burning.

The myth itself is enshrined in that country's Wilderness Act (1964), which defines wilderness as "untrammeled by man" and as "affected primarily by the forces of nature, with the imprint of man's work substantially unnoticed."[9] It is of little surprise that people holding this view of wilderness, and of previous human passivity in relation to it, should eschew active wilderness management in the present, whether through fire or other means. Charles Kay notes that in the case of Yellowstone National Park, this refusal to manage has had significantly deleterious effects. That park "now contains some of the worst overgrazed riparian [riverbank] areas in the nation . . . because park managers and environmentalists refuse to abandon misguided concepts of 'wilderness' and 'natural regulation.'"[10] This has not only affected the flora but also the fauna.[11] Environmentalist activists *have* enthusiastically supported the reintroduction of wolves into the park, which might be expected to help cut down the numbers of the ungulates (e.g., elk) responsible for the overgrazing. However, their settled view of "wilderness" blinds them to the fact that it was Native Americans, and not wolves, who were in the past the ultimate keystone predator. It was they who "once structured Yellowstone and other ecosystems."[12] If there really is a desire to turn the clock back to "the way things were," suggests Kay, then logic implies putting Native Americans back into Yellowstone along with the wolves.

THE END OF THE MATTER

It matters what we believe about the past. It matters that what we believe about the past is actually true. Myths are often comforting, and we may come to feel that we need them. But what we really need, as opposed to what we might feel that we need, is not stories about the past that are at odds with the evidence. Such stories are in the end dangerous—and all the more dangerous because they make us feel good. What we really need is stories about the past that are *consistent* with the evidence. Only such stories can really help us. Only such stories will really contribute to the flourishing of the world in which we live. These are the kinds of stories we need, and these are the kinds of stories that, if we are smart, we should desire.

In chapter 7, when I first wrote of need and desire and their ability to lead us astray in our understanding of the past, I repeated a story told by Alice Ingerson about the student who took her anthropology course because she wanted to learn about primitive peoples living in harmony with nature. When she realized how difficult it was going to be to document this, she confessed that she did not think she wanted to learn what she was going to learn in the class. Ingerson does not tell us whether this student eventually came to understand the foolishness of this first reaction; one hopes that she did. Ingerson does have this to say, however, about the student body as a whole by the end of the semester: "Most students . . . learned a different attitude toward both research and history. Rather than feeling crushed when new facts required revision of their previous theories, they welcomed new information that forced them to build better theories."[13] They learned to take seriously and to embrace the particulars of history—not to impose a theory *upon* the facts, but to allow the facts their own integrity and then to attempt to tell a story that genuinely accounted for all of them. We need not be afraid of evidence. Good stories delight in evidence and thereby provide us insight into the real, the true, the good, and the beautiful.

It is this simple rule with respect to attaining genuine knowledge that has routinely been neglected by those who have become devoted to the concepts of the axial age and the dark green golden age. They have not paid sufficient attention to particulars, which when soberly considered might lead in due course to a faithful, generalized account of what lies behind us. They have instead generalized about the past in pursuit of a story that each group already holds to be true, even though it is, in truth, a fiction. Inconvenient truths have in the process simply been dismissed, and intransigent realities have been distorted, all in the quest for convenient myths. An entirely false consciousness about the ancient condition of humanity has arisen in many quarters as a result, and this false consciousness currently informs all sorts of beliefs, policies, and actions. This is unfortunate, and—as our parents used to tell us about running with scissors—it is not safe. We need to cease believing, and doing, such things.

I recognize that this modest proposal of mine may well fall on deaf ears, for unfortunately we live in a world in which "falsehoods are harder to kill than a Hollywood zombie. Run them through with fact, and still they shamble forward, fueled by echo chamber media, ideological tribalism, cognitive dissonance, a certain imperviousness to shame, and an understanding that a lie repeated long enough, loudly enough, becomes, in the minds of those who need to believe it, truth."[14] Nevertheless, I press the point. To the extent that we are going to ground our present and future lives in the world of the past at all, it needs to be in the world that actually existed, and not in the world that never was.

NOTES

INTRODUCTION

1   I am alluding here to the 2006 documentary *An Inconvenient Truth*, which describes United States vice president Al Gore's campaign to educate people about global warming.

2   Writers on the axial age tend to differ on whether and when they capitalize *axial* and *age*. For the sake of consistency, I shall in this book (except in headings and where I am quoting others) never capitalize either.

3   Bron Taylor, *Dark Green Religion: Nature Spirituality and the Planetary Future* (Berkeley: University of California, 2010).

4   Bobbi S. Low, "Behavioral Ecology of Conservation in Traditional Societies," *Human Nature* 7 (1996): 353–79 (355).

CHAPTER 1

1   Johann P. Arnason, "The Axial Age and Its Interpreters: Reopening a Debate," in Arnason, Eisenstadt and Wittrock, *Axial Civilizations and World History*, 19–49.

2   Karl Jaspers, "The Axial Age of Human History: A Base for the Unity of Mankind," *Commentary* 6 (1948): 430–35. The editors of the journal in which this essay appears inform us that it is a translation from the German, but they do not tell us *of what* it is a translation. It *appears* to be a translation, however, of much of what will appear in the following year as chapter 1 of part 1 of *Vom Ursprung und Ziel der Geschichte* (Zurich: Artemis, 1949), translated later as *The Origin and the Goal of History*, trans. M. Bullock (New Haven, Conn.: Yale University Press, 1953).

3   Jaspers, "Age," 430.

4   Jaspers, "Age," 431, 432, 434.

5   Jaspers, "Age," 434.

6   Jaspers, "Age," 435.

7   Jaspers, *Origin*, 213–14, 226–27, 228. He is, of course, writing against the background of the preceding period of National Socialism in Germany and then the Second World War.

8   We do nevertheless see some embrace of it in the immediately succeeding decades. Indeed, writing in 1975 Arnaldo Momigliano tells us that "it has become commonplace . . . to speak of the *Achsenzeit*, of the axial age. . . . There is a very real element of truth in this formulation." Arnaldo Momigliano, *Alien Wisdom: The Limits of Hellenization* (Cambridge: Cambridge University Press, 1975), 8. See further the various papers in *Daedalus* 104, no. 2 (1975), among them the introductory essay by Benjamin I. Schwartz, "The Age of Transcendence" (1–7).

9   See the World Commission on Global Consciousness and Spirituality website, http://globalspirit.org/, accessed May 5, 2011.

10   Ewert Cousins, "Spirituality in Today's World," in *Religion in Today's World: The Religious Situation of the World from 1945 to the Present Day*, ed. Frank Whaling (Edinburgh: T&T Clark, 1987), 306–34 (307). His first name is misspelled in the book itself as *Ewart*—a common mistake, it seems.

11   Cousins, "Spirituality," 307, 326.

12   Cousins, "Spirituality," 327.

13   Cousins, "Spirituality," 330–31.

14   Cousins, "Spirituality," 331–33. A good example of what this project looks like from Cousins' point of view is found in Ewert H. Cousins, "Male-Female Aspects of the Trinity in Christian Mysticism," in *Sexual Archetypes, East and West*, ed. Bina Gupta (New York: Paragon House, 1987), 37–50. Whereas the new consciousness of the first axial age possessed "male modes of thought and . . . patriarchal priorities," suppressing the feminine, alienating the person from nature and community, and producing an otherworldly attitude (48), in the second axial age "the human community is rediscovering on a global level the female characteristics of the consciousness of the Pre-Axial Period without losing the distinctive male values of Axial consciousness" (49). This requires us to revisit the question of male-female archetypes in the world's religions—something that Cousins himself does in this essay, from the perspective of Christian faith, as he explores "the female dimension of the Trinitarian archetype, bringing this to light through dialogue with other religions in which the feminine has been more prominent than in the West" (49).

15   Cousins, "Spirituality," 334.

16   Wayne Teasdale, "Concluding Reflections: Toward a Second Axial Age," in *Embracing Earth: Catholic Approaches to Ecology*, ed. Albert J. LaChance and John E. Carroll (Maryknoll, N.Y.: Orbis, 1994), 255–75 (263–64, 273–74).

17   Carlton H. Tucker, "From the Axial Age to the New Age: Religion as a Dynamic of World History," *History Teacher* 27 (1994): 449–64 (454, 455).

18   Yves Lambert, "Religion in Modernity as a New Axial Age: Secularization or New Religious Forms?" *Sociology of Religion* 60 (1999): 303–33.

19   Michael H. Barnes, *Stages of Thought: The Co-evolution of Religious Thought and Science* (Oxford: Oxford University Press, 2000), chap. 5. The idea is also fundamental to the account of the rise of Western individualism that is found in Andreas Buss, "The Evolution of Western Individualism," *Religion* 30 (2000): 1–25, who contrasts the "outworldly individualism" of axial age civilizations to our modern "inworldly individualism."

20   Elise Boulding, "An Axial Age? Imagining Peace in the New Millennium," in *Principled World Politics: The Challenge of Normative International Relations*, ed.

Paul Wapner and Lester E. J. Ruiz (Lanham, Md.: Rowman & Littlefield, 2000), 240–49.

21 Gananath Obeyesekere, *Imagining Karma: Ethical Transformation in Amerindian, Buddhist, and Greek Rebirth* (Berkeley: University of California Press, 2002), 75, 115–25.

22 P. Roger Gillette, "A Religion for an Age of Science," *Zygon* 37 (2002): 461–71. From the same year we may note an Internet post by John H. Van Ness, who is described among other things as a senior staff therapist at Monadnock Area Psychotherapy and Spirituality Services in Keene, New Hampshire. Van Ness refers to Ewert Cousins simply as "showing" in his 1992 book *Christ of the 21st Century* (Rockport, Mass.: Element) that "an axial transformation of human consciousness occurred between 800 and 200 B.C.E." He refers to Cousins on the way to arguing that the wise use of cyberspace in this second axial age can contribute to the human evolutionary journey toward our destiny as transpersonal beings. John H. Van Ness, *The Internet and the New Transformation of Consciousness*, October 2002, http://www.vngroup.com/Aoir/John.htm, accessed on May 5, 2011.

23 William E. Herbrechtsmeier, "The Burden of the Axial Age: Transcendentalism in Religion as a Function of Empire," in *Defining Religion: Investigating the Boundaries between the Sacred and Secular*, ed. Arthur Greil and D. Bromley, Religion and the Social Order 10 (Amsterdam: JAI Press, 2003), 109–26.

24 John Hick, *An Interpretation of Religion: Human Responses to the Transcendent*, 2nd ed. (New Haven, Conn.: Yale University Press, 2004).

25 Hick, *Interpretation*, 21–33 (29).

26 Hick, *Interpretation*, 22.

27 Steven G. Smith, *Appeal and Attitude: Prospects for Ultimate Meaning* (Bloomington: Indiana University Press, 2005). In chapter 2 we learn that "all the religions of the 'world religion' type and the classical philosophies are supreme appeal moves geared to command the attention of mentally free individuals" (xi). Chapter 6 discusses attitude as it is expressed in such realities as the benevolence and filial piety of Confucianism, the tranquility of the Upanishads, the devotion in the *Bhagavad Gita*, the reasonableness and civic piety of Greek philosophy, and the righteousness and mercy of Israelite prophecy.

28 Mario Liverani, *Israel's History and the History of Israel*, trans. Chiara Peri and Philip R. Davies (London: Equinox, 2005), chap. 10.

29 William Morrow, "The Affirmation of Divine Righteousness in Early Penitential Prayers: A Sign of Judaism's Entry into the Axial Age," in *The Origins of Penitential Prayer in Second Temple Judaism*, ed. Boda, Falk, and Werline, vol. 1 of *Seeking the Favor of God* (Atlanta: Society of Biblical Literature, 2006). The concept also turns up in the writings of Jürgen Habermas, as noted by Andrew Edgar, *Habermas: The Key Concepts* (London: Routledge, 2006), 57–58. For Habermas, "the ethics of all global civilisations is underpinned by broad conceptions of human autonomy, responsibility and dignity that were established in the axial period (the eighth to the third centuries BCE) in the cultures of China, India, Israel and Greece."

30 Karen Armstrong, *A History of God: The 4000-Year Quest of Judaism, Christianity and Islam* (New York: Knopf, 1994). The axial age plays some part in her reflections in this book on the history of Judaism, Christianity, and Islam, but it does not have the central role that it plays in her later writing and thinking. In *History* it is deployed almost exclusively in her treatment of the development of Israelite monotheism in the eighth century BCE, especially as illustrated in the book of

Isaiah (27–45). It is a relatively minor element within the whole "history of God" (substantially involving both Christianity and Islam) that is commended to us as we seek to "create a vibrant new faith for the twenty-first century" (399). In the two books we are about to consider next, however, the axial age is far more important to Armstrong's thinking.

31   Karen Armstrong, *A Short History of Myth* (Toronto: Knopf, 2005), 41, 79.

32   Armstrong, *Myth*, 80–81.

33   Armstrong, *Myth*, 136–37.

34   Karen Armstrong, *The Great Transformation: The Beginning of Our Religious Traditions* (Toronto: Knopf, 2006), xi–xiv, 390–91, 397.

35   For one Internet example, see John D. Mayer, "Why Did People Change in the Axial Age?" The Personality Analyst, *Psychology Today*, June 15, 2009, http://www.psychologytoday.com/blog/the-personality-analyst/200906/why-did-people-change-in-the-axial-age; accessed on May 5, 2011.

36   Hans Joas, "The Cultural Values of Europe: An Introduction," in *The Cultural Values of Europe*, ed. Hans Joas and Klaus Wiegandt, trans. Alex Skinner (Liverpool: Liverpool University Press, 2008), 1–21 (7).

37   Robert Engelman, *More: Population, Nature and What Women Want* (Washington, D.C.: Island Press, 2008), chap. 6.

38   Hoda Mahmoudi, "The Permanence of Change: Contemporary Sociological and Baha'i Perspectives on Modernity," *The Journal of Baha'i Studies* 18 (2008): 41–76 (46, 47).

39   Mahmoudi, "Permanence," 72–73. See "Axial Age," *New World Encyclopedia*, http://www.newworldencyclopedia.org/entry/Axial_Age, accessed on May 5, 2011, for an example of the axial age being deployed in a similar way by an author advocating the faith of the Unification Church of Rev. Sun Myung Moon.

40   Baruch Halpern, *From Gods to God: The Dynamics of Iron Age Cosmologies*, ed. M. J. Adams, Forschungen zum Alten Testament 63 (Tübingen: Mohr Siebeck, 2009). The introduction and the essays themselves scarcely mention the axial age by name; what is interesting though, is that Jaspers' is the overall framework chosen for their presentation.

41   Mark Muesse, *The Hindu Traditions: A Concise Introduction* (Minneapolis: Fortress, 2011), 62–73 (62).

42   Robert Bellah, *Religion in Human Evolution: From the Paleolithic to the Axial Age* (Cambridge, Mass.: Harvard University Press, 2011).

43   Jaspers, "Age," 430.

CHAPTER 2

1   Arnason, "Age," 26–36.

2   Arnason, "Age," 26.

3   Jaspers, *Origin*, 2.

4   Arnason, "Age," 34.

5   More broadly, Robert Bellah makes the point that all the axial civilizations except China experienced imperial pressure from the Achaemenid Persian Empire (c. 550–330 BCE) at critical moments in their development. Robert N. Bellah, "What Is Axial about the Axial Age?" *European Journal of Sociology* 46 (2005): 69–89 (75).

6   Arnason, "Age," 34–36.

7   Jaspers, *Origin*, 8. Emphasis in original.

8   Arnason, "Age," 36.

9   Eric Voegelin, *Order and History*, 5 vols. (Baton Rouge: Louisiana State

University Press, 1956–1987). On Voegelin's relationship to Eisenstadt see further Glenn Hughes, Stephen A. McKnight, and Geoffrey L. Price, eds., *Politics, Order and History: Essays on the Work of Eric Voegelin* (Sheffield: Sheffield Academic, 2001), in which the judgment is entered (in the introduction by McKnight, 17–46) that "Eisenstadt's studies . . . confirm and expand Voegelin's analysis of modern Western civilization as deriving from religious impulses that contain immanentized forms of apocalypticism and Gnosticism" (23).

10   Shmuel N. Eisenstadt, "The Axial Age Breakthroughs: Their Characteristics and Origins," in *The Origin and Diversity of Axial Age Civilizations*, ed. S. N. Eisenstadt (Albany: State University of New York Press, 1986), 1–28 (1, 3).

11   See further other contributions by Eisenstadt, such as his earlier "The Axial Age: The Emergence of Transcendental Visions and the Rise of Clerics," *European Journal of Sociology* 23 (1982): 294–314; and his later *Fundamentalism, Sectarianism, and Revolution: The Jacobin Dimension of Modernity* (Cambridge: Cambridge University Press, 1999).

12   Arnason, "Age," 40, 41, 43–44.

13   Arnason, "Age," 44.

14   Eisenstadt, "Breakthroughs," 8.

15   Arnason, "Age," 47.

16   Arnason, "Age," 48.

17   A summary of the paper is posted at Johann Arnason, "Re-historicizing the Axial Age," Central European University Department of History website, http://history.ceu.hu/events/2011-01-12/re-historicizing-the-axial-age, accessed on May 9, 2011.

18   Eisenstadt, *Fundamentalism*, 7, 13.

19   Eisenstadt, *Fundamentalism*, 4. The same is actually true of Christianity, of course, although Eisenstadt does not draw attention to this fact.

20   Eisenstadt, *Fundamentalism*, 14–38.

21   Eisenstadt, *Fundamentalism*, 15, 16–17, 19.

22   Voegelin, *Order*, 2:3–4, 23.

23   Voegelin, *Order*, 2:23.

24   Voegelin, *Order*, 2:21–22.

25   Voegelin, *Order*, 4:3.

26   Voegelin, *Order*, 4:3–4.

27   Voegelin, *Order*, 4:4–5. Reviewing the fate of Moses, in particular, in his slide down "the time scale of meaning" in Jaspers and his predecessors, Voegelin drily notes, "Moses is a somewhat ubiquitous figure as a disturber of the constructivist peace" (5n1).

28   Voegelin, *Order*, 4:5.

29   Arnason, "Age," 48n51, referring to Stefan Breuer, "Kulturen der Achsenzeit: Leistung und Grenzen eines geschichtsphilosophischen Konzepts," *Saeculum* 45 (1994): 1–33.

30   Breuer, "Kulturen," 33. The translations of Breuer are my own.

31   Barnes, *Stages*, 90–92.

32   Theodore M. Ludwig, *The Sacred Paths: Understanding the Religions of the World*, 4th ed. (Upper Saddle River, N.J.: Pearson Prentice Hall, 2006), 334. For a helpful summary of the data relevant to the dating see Shaul Shaked, "Zoroastrian Origins: Indian and Iranian connections," in Arnason, Eisenstadt, and Wittrock, *Axial Civilizations and World History*, 183–200 (183–89). Shaked himself opts for an eighth- or ninth-century date for Zoroaster.

33   Obeyesekere, *Imagining Karma*, xiii, 75, 115–25.

CHAPTER 3

1   Hick, *Interpretation*, 29–30. Note further on this point Voegelin, *Order*, 4:47–58, who explains in volume 4 why his book project as originally conceived (and unpacked in volumes 1–3) has been abandoned by the time he is writing the present volume (published in 1974). He tells us of his fresh realization that the notion of unilinear history (previously associated by him with Israel as a new, axial-like phenomenon) had, in fact, already existed previously in cultures defined by the cosmological myth, and indeed that the myth itself survived the spiritual outbursts in which he is so interested.

2   Hick, *Interpretation*, 31.

3   Hick, *Interpretation*, 31.

4   For a similarly crassly inaccurate statement, see Gillette, "Age of Science," 462: "Students of the history of philosophy and religion have noted that all of the current major world philosophic and religious traditions emerged in roughly 800–200 B.C.E., a period of creative and radical cultural change that is being called an axial age or period." All of them . . . with the tiny exceptions of the important ones that did not!

5   I do not dispute that Judaism evolved over time into its current form. What I see no reason at all to believe is that Mosaic Yahwism in its essential core elements did not predate the time of the Israelite prophets. Nor did the prophets themselves believe this.

6   The significance in axial terms of the centuries CE rather than BCE for China must also be considered. Note the statement (which also touches upon the importance of Christianity in the West) near the end of Christoph Harbsmeier's informative essay "The Axial Millennium in China," in Arnason, Eisenstadt, and Wittrock, *Axial Civilizations and World History*, 469–507 (501): "The decisive break occurred in China, and with remarkable simultaneity in the West, during the first millennium CE [not BCE!], when Buddhism in China and Christianity in the West profoundly changed the intellectual and cultural landscape."

7   Hick, *Interpretation*, 34n6.

8   It is specifically in the context of the history of ancient India that David Shulman pronounces as problematic in the axial age discussion "the prevalent language of rupture, disruption, and breakthrough, to say nothing of notions of 'transcendence' and the breakdown of an alleged archaic homology between domains. Such formulations, conspicuous in Jaspers, are strikingly Western." David Shulman, "Axial Grammar," in Arnason, Eisenstadt, and Wittrock, *Axial Civilizations and World History*, 369–95 (369–70).

9   Sheldon Pollock, "Axialism and Empire," in Arnason, Eisenstadt, and Wittrock, *Axial Civilizations and World History*, 397–450 (397–98).

10   Bellah, "Age," 69. In *Religion* he does exclude consideration of Christianity and Islam as falling "outside the temporal parameters of this book" (599).

11   Merlin Donald, *Origins of the Modern Mind: Three Stages in the Evolution of Culture and Cognition* (Cambridge, Mass.: Harvard University Press, 1991). In the first transition our hominid ancestors acquired mimetic skill (the ability to represent knowledge through voluntary motor acts), and in the second, speech, which allowed Homo sapiens to develop complex, preliterate culture. In the third transition, symbolic systems emerged, ranging from cuneiforms, hieroglyphics, and ideograms to alphabetic languages and mathematics.

12   Bellah, "Age," 71–72, 77–78.

13   Bellah, "Age," 72, 83, 86.

14   Jan Assmann, *God and the Gods: Egypt, Israel and the Rise of Monotheism* (Madison: University of Wisconsin Press, 2008), 79.

15   Assmann, *God*, 80–83.

16   Assmann, *God*, 81, 83, 86, 89. For a series of reflections on the axial age hypothesis from the perspective of ancient *Mesopotamian* rather than Egyptian civilization, see Piotr Michalowski, "Mesopotamian Vistas on Axial Transformations," in Arnason, Eisenstadt, and Wittrock, *Axial Civilizations and World History*, 157–81.

17   Bellah, "Age," 88–89.

18   Bellah, *Religion*, 283, 321, 323.

19   Bellah, *Religion*, 356, 379, 383, 391, 395.

20   Bellah, "Age," 89.

21   See also James A. Montmarquet, "Jaspers, the Axial Age, and Christianity," *American Catholic Philosophical Quarterly* 83 (2009): 239–54 (253), who provides a quotation to this effect for the first epigraph of our chapter. He does so in the course of his own argument advocating for a clear distinction between an axial age in India and China, on the one hand, and an axial age marked by Western monotheism, on the other. Procrustes is a robber of Greek legend who stretched out or mutilated his victims in order to make them fit the length of his bed. Confucius and Isaiah are, in this case, the victims.

22   Peter Wagner, "Palomar's Questions: The Axial Age Hypothesis, European Modernity and Historical Contingency," in Arnason, Eisenstadt, and Wittrock, *Axial Civilizations and World History*, 87–106.

23   Armstrong, *Myth*, 60.

24   The *city* of Jerusalem is after all the very focal point of worship of God throughout much of the tradition, and there is no rejection of musical instruments in the tradition, even though Cain's descendant Jubal is implicated in their invention.

25   James L. Crenshaw, "Job, Book of," in *The Anchor Bible Dictionary*, ed. David Noel Freedman (New York: Doubleday, 1996), 3:864–65.

26   Armstrong, *Myth*, 81.

27   Simon Goldhill, "The Wisdom of the Ancients," *New Statesman* 18.883 (October 31, 2005), 48–50.

28   Armstrong, *Transformation*, xiii–xiv.

29   Armstrong, *Transformation*, xiv–xv, xvii–xviii.

30   Armstrong, *Transformation*, 171–72.

31   Armstrong, *Transformation*, 390–91.

32   John Wilson, "Roots of Faith," review of *The Great Transformation*, by Karen Armstrong, *New York Times*, April 30, 2006, http://www.nytimes.com/2006/04/30/books/review/30wilson.html, accessed on May 13, 2011.

33   Diarmaid MacCulloch, "The Axis of Goodness," *Guardian*, March 17, 2006, http://www.guardian.co.uk/books/2006/mar/18/highereducation.news.

34   Jaspers, "Age," 433.

CHAPTER 4

1   John Zerzan, *Twilight of the Machines* (Port Townsend, Wash.: Feral House, 2008).

2   The title of his sixteenth chapter, in fact, is precisely "Finding Our Way Back Home."

3   Zerzan, *Twilight*, 124.

4   Note the title of chapter 4: "The Iron Grip of Civilization: The Axial Age."

5   Zerzan, *Twilight*, 28, 36.

6   Zerzan, *Twilight*, 36–37, 124–25.
7   Taylor, *Religion*, 5.
8   Taylor, *Religion*, ix.
9   Taylor, *Religion*, 9.
10   Taylor, *Religion*, 10. I cite this material because it captures well some of the key aspects of dark green religion, but it is in fact debatable how far Rousseau may rightly be thought of as a key spiritual ancestor of dark green religionists. It is common for him to be so regarded, both by the proponents of the movement and by those who oppose the notion of the noble savage with which they identify him. However, Arthur O. Lovejoy pointed out some time ago that Rousseau himself did not believe that an ideal condition of human society ever existed in the past and that he never himself used the term *le bon sauvage*. Arthur O. Lovejoy, "The Supposed Primitivism of Rousseau's Discourse on Inequality," *Modern Philology* 21 (1923): 165–86 (esp. 183–85). Various authors have repeated these caveats, beginning with Hoxie Neale Fairchild in a book of the same time period, *The Noble Savage: A Study in Romantic Naturalism* (New York: Columbia University Press, 1928). For a brief survey and his own further commentary, see Ter Ellingson, *The Myth of the Noble Savage* (Berkeley: University of California Press, 2001), 1–4, 80–95. According to Tzvetan Todorov (cited by Ellingson on pp. 3–4), "Rousseau's thought is traditionally associated with primitivism and the cult of the noble savage. In reality . . . Rousseau was actually a vigilant critic of these tendencies."
11   Taylor, *Religion*, 13–41.
12   Taylor, *Religion*, 19.
13   Cited in Taylor, *Religion*, 20.
14   Cited in Taylor, *Religion*, 36.
15   Taylor, *Religion*, 42.
16   Cited in Taylor, *Religion*, 52.
17   Taylor, *Religion*, 72–73, 75.
18   Taylor, *Religion*, 78–79, referring to Daniel Quinn, *Ishmael: A Novel* (New York: Bantam, 1992).
19   Taylor, *Religion*, 91, 99, 101.
20   Cited in Taylor, *Religion*, 100.
21   Cited in Taylor, *Religion*, 103. Surfing can, Melekian opined, "make one more compassionate toward both people and nature" (104).
22   Taylor, *Religion*, 147, 154, 180, 217.
23   Indeed, he uses many quotations in this book from his previous books.
24   David Suzuki, *The Legacy: An Elder's Vision for Our Sustainable Future* (Vancouver: Greystone Books, 2010), 19, 36.
25   Suzuki, *Legacy*, 58, 71, 83, 86, 89, 96.
26   Suzuki, *Legacy*, 55.
27   Suzuki, *Legacy*, 86, 94.
28   Cited in Suzuki, *Legacy*, 84.
29   Note, e.g., David Suzuki, *The Sacred Balance: Rediscovering Our Place in Nature* (Vancouver: Greystone Books, 1997), 12–15.
30   Note, e.g., Suzuki, *Balance*, 184–88.
31   Peter Knudtson and David Suzuki, *Wisdom of the Elders* (Toronto: Stoddart, 1992), 9.
32   Knudtson and Suzuki, *Wisdom*, 9.
33   Suzuki, *Balance*, 190–91. It is not entirely clear how many of the four religions he has in mind.

34 Knudtson and Suzuki, *Wisdom*, 13–16 (13).
35 Knudtson and Suzuki, *Wisdom*, 16.
36 Knudtson and Suzuki, *Wisdom*, xxvii–xxviii, 185–86.
37 Derrick Jensen, *Endgame*, vol. 1, *The Problem of Civilization* (New York: Seven Stories, 2006). The second volume is subtitled *Resistance*.
38 Jensen, *Endgame*, 1:17–18, 35–36, 283.
39 Jensen, *Endgame*, 1:69, 75, 92, 93.
40 Jensen, *Endgame*, 1:38.
41 Jensen, *Endgame*, 1:52. See also p. 94: "the lives of traditional indigenous peoples the world over are far more full of leisure and play than ours."
42 Jensen, *Endgame*, 1:39–40, 105–6, 164, 186.
43 Jensen, *Endgame*, 1:38, 40, 92, 104–5.
44 Jensen, *Endgame*, 1:22–23, 29, 32, 89, 186, 226, 233, 285.
45 Jensen, *Endgame*, 1:221–27.
46 Jensen, *Endgame*, 1:227, 301.
47 Taylor, *Religion*, 183–84.

CHAPTER 5

1   See, e.g., Robert J. Wenke, *Patterns in Prehistory: Humankind's First Three Million Years*, 4th ed. (New York: Oxford University Press, 1999), 160–239.
2   Wenke, *Patterns*, 268–330.
3   Robert L. Kelly, *The Foraging Spectrum: Diversity in Hunter-Gatherer Lifeways* (Washington, D.C.: Smithsonian Institution Press, 1995), 7.
4   Lewis Henry Morgan, *Ancient Society: Researches in the Lines of Human Progress from Savagery Through Barbarism to Civilization* (New York: Henry Holt, 1877).
5   Kelly, *Spectrum*, 9.
6   Kelly, *Spectrum*, 15.
7   Kelly, *Spectrum*, 18.
8   Thomas Hobbes, *Leviathan*, ed. Michael Oakeshott (Oxford: Basil Blackwell, 1946), 82.
9   Harry Levin, *The Myth of the Golden Age in the Renaissance* (Bloomington: Indiana University Press, 1969).
10 See further Ellingson, *Myth*, 11–41 (p. 36 for the quotation from Dryden).
11 Paul Hazard, *The European Mind (1680–1715)* (London: Hollis and Carter, 1953), 14. See further Ellingson, *Myth*, 64–76.
12 Ellingson, *Myth*, 290–302, finds the originating point of the full-blown myth itself not in the work of Rousseau (as has commonly been thought) but in "the works of advocates of racial inequality and hierarchical domination" in the nineteenth century, specifically those of "a racist faction in the Ethnological Society of London" (238). These people projected the myth onto Rousseau in order then to mock it, in pursuit of their own agendas with respect to racial superiority and dominance.
13 Kelly, *Spectrum*, 24–25.
14 Kelly, *Spectrum*, 27, quoting Headland and Reid.
15 Steven LeBlanc, *Constant Battles: The Myth of the Peaceful, Noble Savage* (New York: St. Martin's Press, 2003), 115 (see further pp. 119–23).
16 LeBlanc, *Battles*, 116–18.
17 LeBlanc, *Battles*, 125–26.
18 LeBlanc, *Battles*, chap. 4.
19 LeBlanc, *Battles*, chaps. 6–7.

20   LeBlanc, *Battles*, 150–51.

21   LeBlanc, *Battles*, 151–53.

22   Paul S. Martin and Christine R. Szuter, "Revising the 'Wild West': Big Game Meets the Ultimate Keystone Species," in Redman et al., *Archaeology of Global Change*, 63–88 (82).

23   Martin and Szuter, "Wild West," 80.

24   It would be a simple matter to multiply examples of such native violence; note, e.g., Jared Diamond's disturbing account of the 1835 Maori assault on the Chatham Islands, in *Guns, Germs and Steel: The Fates of Human Societies* (New York: Norton, 1997), 53–57.

25   LeBlanc, *Battles*, 6.

26   LeBlanc, *Battles*, 8.

27   LeBlanc, *Battles*, 14–15. The connection between conflict and the gobbling up of resources is well illustrated by the far from ecologically wise prehistoric peoples who settled Easter Island in the second half of the first millennium CE. They proceeded both to multiply to the very limits of the island's carrying capacity and to devastate both its flora and its fauna. This led in turn to resource depletion in the centuries preceding European contact, which in turn led to "pervasive and brutal intertribal warfare," including cannibalism. See Patrick V. Kirch, "Oceanic Islands: Microcosms of 'Global Change,'" in Redman et al., *Archaeology of Global Change*, 13–27 (16).

28   Thomas Headland, "Revisionism in Ecological Anthropology," *Current Anthropology* 38 (1997): 605–9 (607).

29   Headland, "Revisionism," 607.

30   See further Steven Pinker, *The Better Angels of Our Nature: Why Violence Has Declined* (New York: Penguin, 2011), 2–4, 31–58.

31   Kelly, *Spectrum*, 293.

32   Kelly, *Spectrum*, 303–4, 328.

33   Kelly, *Spectrum*, 298.

34   Kelly, *Spectrum*, 329–30.

CHAPTER 6

1   Allyn MacLean Stearman, "Only Slaves Climb Trees: Revisiting the Myth of the Ecologically Noble Savage in Amazonia," *Human Nature* 5 (1994): 339–57.

2   Stearman, "Slaves," 347–48.

3   Stearman, "Slaves," 351–52.

4   Cited from "Interview with Nicanor González: We Are Not Conservationists; Indigenous Organizations Are Working at Every Level—Local, National, and International," *Cultural Survival Quarterly* 16, no. 3 (1992), http://www.culturalsurvival.org/publications/cultural-survival-quarterly/colombia/interview-nicanor-gonzalez-we-are-not-conservation, accessed February 8, 2012; these lines are also partially cited in Stearman, "Slaves," 352. González was one of the founders of Project PEMASKEY, which since 1983 has managed a forestry park in the Kuna homeland. He was also international coordinator for the Second Interamerican Indian Congress on Natural Resources and the Environment, held in Bolivia in 1991.

5   Cited in Low, "Ecology," 372. Note further the story told (and his comments on it) by Joseph Epes Brown, a Chippewa-Cree, in his *Teaching Spirits: Understanding Native American Religious Traditions*, with Emily Cousins (New York: Oxford University Press, 2001), 85–86.

6   Michael S. Alvard, "Testing the 'Ecologically Noble Savage' Hypothesis: Inter-specific Prey Choice by Piro Hunters in Amazonian Peru," *Human Ecology* 21 (1993): 355–87 (356).

7   Foraging theorists study the ways in which animals search out and exploit food resources in their particular environments. They are especially interested in how the animals strategize in order to maximize their energy intake in relation to the time they spend foraging. See, e.g., David W. Stephens and John R. Krebs, *Foraging Theory*, Monographs in Behavior and Ecology (Princeton, N.J.: Princeton University Press, 1986).

8   Since the tapir is rare and mainly nocturnal, however, it was not often encountered.

9   Alvard, "Testing," 370, 378–80.

10   Alvard, "Testing," 384.

11   For example, seals, who only bear one pup at a time, were nevertheless killed along with their pups.

12   Atholl Anderson, "A Fragile Plenty: Pre-European Māori and the New Zealand Environment," in *Environmental Histories of New Zealand*, ed. Eric Pawson and Tom Brooking (Melbourne: Oxford University Press, 2002), 19–34 (28, 29).

13   Anderson, "Plenty," 32–34.

14   Kirch, "Islands," 15.

15   Michael S. Alvard, "Evolutionary Theory, Conservation and Human Environmental Impact," in Kay and Simmons, *Wilderness and Political Ecology*, 28–43 (29, 30).

16   Charles E. Kay, "Are Ecosystems Structured from the Top-Down or Bottom-Up?" in Kay and Simmons, *Wilderness and Political Ecology*, 215–37 (215).

17   Human impact is disputed, for example, by Jack M. Broughton, "Pre-Columbian Human Impact on California Vertebrates: Evidence from Old Bones and Implications for Wilderness Policy," in Kay and Simmons, *Wilderness and Political Ecology*, 44–71 (66–68). The response by Charles E. Kay in the same volume, however, is cogent. He argues that it does not require very many new Paleo-Indians to cause the entire ecosystem, which already possesses other predators that are keeping herbivore numbers low, to change radically. Charles E. Kay, "Afterword: False Gods, Ecological Myths, and Biological Reality," 238–61. The theory of Pleistocene overkill in North America is certainly consistent with the data provided by Paul S. Martin in his "Prehistoric Extinctions: In the Shadow of Man" (same volume, 1–27). He describes large numbers of extinctions worldwide among large terrestrial mammals during the last 40,000 years, noting that whatever caused these extinctions had no impact on large mammals in the oceans and refuting the idea that the cause was climate change. Diamond, *Guns, Germs and Steel*, 43, puts the matter very sharply with respect to the extinction of large mammals specifically in Australia: "Personally, I can't fathom why Australia's giants should have survived innumerable droughts in their tens of millions of years of Australian history, and then have chosen to drop dead almost simultaneously (at least on a time scale of millions of years) precisely and just coincidentally when the first humans arrived."

18   Martin and Szuter, "Wild West," 64.

19   Kay, "Ecosystems," 225.

20   Martin and Szuter, "Wild West," 82.

21   Cited in Broughton, "Impact," 45.

22   On this point and all others to do with Paleo-Indians and the buffalo, see

Shepard Krech III, *The Ecological Indian: Myth and History* (New York: Norton, 1999), 121–49. He further discusses (in his chapter 6) the way in which "Indians hunted white-tailed deer to extreme scarcity and even to local extinction" (163); and the way in which, among the native peoples studied in his chapter 7 with respect to the hunting of beavers, "the concept of conservation seems to have been largely absent" in the seventeenth and eighteenth centuries.

23 Gerald Williams, "Aboriginal Use of Fire: Are There Any 'Natural' Plant Communities?" in Kay and Simmons, *Wilderness and Political Ecology*, 179–214.

24 Krech, *Indian*, 101.

25 Williams, "Fire," 207.

26 Steve Pyne, quoted in Williams, "Fire," 185.

27 Krech, *Indian*, 101.

28 Daniel Botkin, quoted in Williams, "Fire," 182.

29 Williams, "Fire," 181. The manipulation was not only by means of fire. As Williams notes on the same page, "there is extensive documentation of tribes changing water flow (canals), practicing farming, grazing." See further Michael Williams, *Americans and Their Forests: A Historical Geography* (Cambridge: Cambridge University Press, 1989), esp. 22–49. On pp. 32–33 Williams says this:

> By the time European man landed on the eastern shores of America, portions of the woodlands were in the process of being changed to a more open, park-like vegetation, largely through the agency of Indian agriculture and the use of fire for clearing and hunting. Much of the "natural" forest remained, but the forest was not the vast, silent, unbroken, impenetrable and dense tangle of trees beloved by many writers in their romantic accounts of the forest wilderness. . . . [T]he Indians had been there in large numbers for millennia before them [the Europeans], and the Indians had been burning, clearing and collecting, and otherwise changing the forest. The impact of the Indian on the forest has not been readily admitted by historians, in much the same way as it has been ignored by plant ecologists of the past.

30 Kay, "Ecosystems," 234.

31 Low, "Ecology," 353, 356, 368.

32 Thomas W. Neumann, "The Role of Prehistoric Peoples in Shaping Ecosystems in the Eastern United States: Implications for Restoration Ecology and Wilderness Management," in Kay and Simmons, *Wilderness and Political Ecology*, 141–78 (143).

33 Low, "Ecology," 353. Emphasis added.

34 Low, "Ecology," 360.

35 Krech, *Indian*, 163–71. See further Flora Lu Holt on the Siona-Secoya of Ecuador: "In their belief system, the Siona-Secoya viewed the forest as a vast habitat with abundant and ultimately inexhaustible resources. In recounting one myth, a respected elder shaman recounted the transformation of man into the tapir and said 'There will always be tapirs. They will never end.' . . . [H]unting was not a threat to animal populations because they could be increased through supernatural means." Flora Lu Holt, "The Catch-22 of Conservation: Indigenous Peoples, Biologists and Cultural Change," *Human Ecology* 33 (2005): 199–215 (208–9).

36 William Wordsworth, *Selected Poetry*, ed. Mark Van Doren (New York: Modern Library, 1950), 82–83.

37 Caspar David Friedrich (1774–1840) was responsible for many well-known romantic paintings, perhaps the most famous of which is his *Wanderer above the Sea of Fog* (*Der Wanderer über dem Nebelmeer*, 1818).

38 See, e.g., Wenke, *Patterns*, 337: "Hunter-gatherers of the recent and contemporary world are probably uncertain guides to what life was like during the millennia when all of our ancestors lived this way."

39 Kelly, *Spectrum*, 337.

40 Cited in Ellingson, *Myth*, 81.

41 Headland, "Revisionism," 606.

CHAPTER 7

1 Alice E. Ingerson, "Comments on Thomas Headland's 'Revisionism in Ecological Anthropology,'" *Current Anthropology* 38 (1997): 615–16 (616).

2 I do not claim, of course, that there are no other factors. To desire and need we should certainly add intellectual laziness, for example. It is simply a fact of academic life that once a concept gets to be referenced by a sufficient number of people, it begins to be referenced by more and more people just because it is "out there," and not necessarily because of its intrinsic merits, which may well not be much considered by these later writers. In such a way bad ideas as well as good ones can easily come to be accorded an almost canonical status—at least for a time. So it is, for example, that "everyone just knows" that Jean-Jacques Rousseau originated the concept of the noble savage (Ellingson, *Myth*, 1–4).

3 Jaspers, "Age," 430, 435.

4 Karl Jaspers and Rudolf Bultmann, *Die Frage der Entmythologisierung* (Munich: Piper, 1954), 103, cited in Voegelin, *Order*, 4:311n5.

5 Voegelin, *Order*, 4:312.

6 Cousins, *Spirituality*, 327, 329–30, 333–34.

7 Armstrong, *Transformation*, xi–xii, xiv, xviii.

8 Armstrong, *Transformation*, 390, 392, 397.

9 Armstrong, *Transformation*, xii–xiii.

10 Jessica Roemischer, "A New Axial Age: Karen Armstrong on the History—and the Future—of God," *EnlightenNext*, http://www.enlightennext.org/magazine/j31/armstrong.asp, accessed on May 20, 2011.

11 Ellingson, *Myth*, 238.

12 Jensen, *Endgame*, 1:41.

13 So, e.g., Jensen, *Endgame*, 2:676–77:
It has always seemed clear to me that violent and nonviolent approaches to social change are complementary. No one I know who advocates the possibility of armed resistance to the dominant culture's degradation and exploitation rejects nonviolent resistance. Many of us routinely participate in nonviolent resistance. . . . [But] our survival really does depend on us learning how to "take our differences"—including violent and nonviolent approaches to stopping civilization from killing the planet—"and make them strengths."

14 Jensen, *Endgame*, 1:186.

15 Jensen, *Endgame*, 1:38, 52, 92, 164.

16 Suzuki, *Legacy*, 83, 89.

17 Knudtson and Suzuki, *Wisdom*, 185.

18 Knudtson and Suzuki, *Wisdom*, xv–xviii.

19 Knudtson and Suzuki, *Wisdom*, xvi.

20 Knudtson and Suzuki, *Wisdom*, xviii–xix.

21 Krech, *Indian*, 75.

22 Ellingson, *Myth*, 68–76.

23 Headland, "Revisionism," 607.

24 E.g., Jensen, *Endgame*, 1:52, 94. Note further the mistaken notion of indigenous warfare as "play" on p. 164.

25 LeBlanc, *Battles*, 3.

CHAPTER 8

1 Even in cultures like the Natufian of the Levant, where grave goods are infrequent, "some burials indicate concern with the philosophical implications of death." Wenke, *Patterns*, 293.

2 See Rodney Stark, *Discovering God: The Origins of the Great Religions and the Evolution of Belief* (New York: HarperOne, 2007), 21–63 (chap. 1, titled "Gods in Primitive Societies").

3 Wenke, *Patterns*, 331–85, and throughout the succeeding chapters.

4 I say "crucially" because I do not agree with Robert Bellah and others that "any distinction between history and prehistory is arbitrary" (*Religion*, xi). We have far more secure access to the past when we have texts than when we do not. In the absence of attention to texts, indeed, our *representations of the past* can all too easily become arbitrary—simply a reflection of our need "to find what at the moment our culture wants to find" (*Religion*, 475).

5 Many sources might be cited for what follows. A good starting point would be John Walton, *Ancient Near Eastern Thought and the Old Testament: Introducing the Conceptual World of the Hebrew Bible* (Grand Rapids: Baker Academic, 2006), whom I cite and refer to frequently below. See also Jean Bottéro, *Religion in Ancient Mesopotamia*, trans. Teresa Lavender Fagan (Chicago: University of Chicago Press, 2001); Stark, *Discovering God*, 43–112; and Daniel C. Snell, *Religions of the Ancient Near East* (Cambridge: Cambridge University Press, 2011).

6 Walton, *Thought*, 87–97.

7 Walton, *Thought*, 103–4.

8 Walton, *Thought*, 115, 119–22, 127–28, 275.

9 Stark, *Discovering God*, 72, quotes Plato (from *The Statesman*) with respect to the later, but similar, Greek situation: priests, says Plato, "understand how to offer our gifts to the gods in sacrifices in a manner pleasing to them, and they know, too, the right forms of prayer for petitioning the gods to bestow blessings on their worshippers."

10 Walton, *Thought*, 136. For similar daily rituals from Egypt, see the text in *Context of Scripture*, 1:34 which describes the care of Amun-Re.

11 Walton, *Thought*, 137.

12 Walton, *Thought*, 279, 281, 283.

13 Walton, *Thought*, 143–44.

14 Walton, *Thought*, 144–49, 239–74, 302–11.

15 Walton, *Thought*, 325.

16 Walton, *Thought*, 318–19.

17 Walton, *Thought*, 215.

18 Stark, *Discovering God*, 112.

19 Variation across the ancient Near East is already perceptible in what I have said so far, as I have noted both the similarities and differences between Mesopotamia and Egypt. We must also allow, of course, for variation *within* Mesopotamia and *within* Egypt, even given an overall climate of changelessness (e.g., we must account for Akhenaten in Egypt, as we saw in chapter 3).

20 Wenke, *Patterns*, 484–513.

21 Wenke, *Patterns*, 514–35 (523).

22   John Boardman, "Greek Art and Architecture," in Boardman, Griffin, and Murray, *Oxford History of the Classical World*, 275–309 (280).

23   Walter Burkert, *The Orientalizing Revolution: Near Eastern Influence on Greek Culture in the Early Archaic Age*, trans. Margaret E. Pinder and Walter Burkert (Cambridge, Mass.: Harvard University Press, 1992), 129. See also Jasper Griffin, "Greek Myth and Hesiod," in Boardman, Griffin, and Murray, *Oxford History of the Classical World*, 78–98 (90–91), who says of the opening of the *Theogony* that "the story is a version of a very archaic one. . . . Its ultimate origin seems to have been Sumerian. . . . Oriental influence, then, is certain for an important myth in Hesiod."

24   Reijer Hooykaas, *Religion and the Rise of Modern Science* (Vancouver: Regent College, 2007), 3.

25   Robert Parker, "Greek Religion," in Boardman, Griffin, and Murray, *Oxford History of the Classical World*, 254–74 (254).

CHAPTER 9

1   Armstrong, *Myth*, 60, 81–83.

2   Armstrong, *Myth*, 83.

3   Armstrong, *Transformation*, xii–xiv.

4   Armstrong, *Transformation*, 170.

5   Lynn White, "The Historical Roots of Our Ecologic Crisis," *Science* 155 (1967): 1203–7. This essay was conveniently reproduced in I. G. Barbour, ed., *Western Man and Environmental Ethics* (Reading: Addison-Wesley, 1973), 18–30, whose page numbers are cited below.

6   White, "Crisis," 25.

7   White, "Crisis," 29.

8   Walton, *Thought*, 87–92 (88), 188–90.

9   I pass over for the sake of space, for example, White's comment about Eve being an afterthought in Genesis 2. He is quite mistaken about this as well. Genesis 2 explicitly describes the situation prior to the woman's creation as "not good," clearly indicating that we have not yet reached, at this point, the state of creation in which everything is "good" (Genesis 1). Solitude for the earth creature was never God's plan, and this problem is fixed as the creation moves toward its final shape. It is clear, then, that we are not meant to read Genesis 2 as following on, chronologically, from Genesis 1, but as a parallel account of creation with its own distinctive interests—one of which concerns the essentially social nature of human beings.

10   Evelyn Stokes, "Māori, Pākehā, and a Tenurial Revolution," in *Environmental Histories of New Zealand*, ed. Eric Pawson and Tom Brooking (Melbourne: Oxford University Press, 2002), 35–51 (35).

11   Jensen, *Endgame*, 1:118, 233–34.

12   Jensen, *Endgame*, 1:160.

13   Jensen, *Endgame*, 1:285.

14   Ludwig, *Paths*, 76–78, 96–100, 148–55.

15   W. K. C. Guthrie, *A History of Greek Philosophy*, vol. 1, *The Earlier Presocratics and the Pythagoreans* (Cambridge: Cambridge University Press, 1962).

16   Eric Voegelin, *Plato* (Baton Rouge: Louisiana State University Press, 1957).

17   David J. Levy, "The Religion of Light: On Mani and Manichaeism," in Arnason, Eisenstadt, and Wittrock, *Axial Civilizations and World History*, 319–36.

18   Ludwig, *Paths*, 389.

19   Iain Provan, *Seriously Dangerous Religion: What the Old Testament Really Says and Why It Matters* (Waco, Tex.: Baylor University Press, 2014).

CHAPTER 10

1   Alasdair MacIntyre, *After Virtue: A Study in Moral Theory* (Notre Dame, Ind.: University of Notre Dame Press, 1981), 216.
2   Kay, "Afterword," 260.
3   Stearman, *Slaves*, 351–52.
4   Ingerson, "Comments," 615.
5   Holt, "Catch-22," 205–6, 209.
6   Holt, "Catch-22," 202, 209.
7   W. T. Vickers, cited in Holt, "Catch-22," 209.
8   Williams, "Fire," 198–200, 207.
9   Cited in Krech, *Indian*, 122.
10   Kay, "Afterword," 259.
11   "Today . . . beaver are ecologically extinct on Yellowstone's northern range because the park's resource-limited ungulates, through repeated browsing, have eliminated the tall willows and aspen beaver need for food." Kay, "Ecosystems," 222.
12   Kay, "Afterword," 260.
13   Ingerson, "Comments," 616.
14   Leonard Pitts Jr., "When Lies Triumph over Facts, We're Done," *Miami Herald*, June 30, 2012, http://www.miamiherald.com/2012/06/30/2876574/when-lies -triumph-over-facts-were.html, accessed on September 7, 2012.

Bibliography

Alvard, Michael S. "Evolutionary Theory, Conservation and Human Environmental Impact." In Kay and Simmons, *Wilderness and Political Ecology*, 28–43.

———. "Testing the 'Ecologically Noble Savage' Hypothesis: Interspecific Prey Choice by Piro Hunters in Amazonian Peru," *Human Ecology* 21 (1993): 355–87.

Anderson, Atholl. "A Fragile Plenty: Pre-European Māori and the New Zealand Environment." In *Environmental Histories of New Zealand*, edited by Eric Pawson and Tom Brooking, 19–34. Melbourne: Oxford University Press, 2002.

Armstrong, Karen. *The Great Transformation: The Beginning of Our Religious Traditions*. Toronto: Knopf, 2006.

———. *A History of God: The 4000-Year Quest of Judaism, Christianity and Islam*. New York: Knopf, 1994.

———. *A Short History of Myth*. Toronto: Knopf, 2005.

Arnason, Johann P. "The Axial Age and Its Interpreters: Reopening a Debate." In Arnason, Eisenstadt, and Wittrock, *Axial Civilizations and World History*, 19–49.

———. "Re-historicizing the Axial Age." Central European University Department of History website. http://history.ceu.hu/events/2011-01-12/re-historicizing-the-axial-age, accessed on May 9, 2011.

Arnason, Johann P., S. N. Eisenstadt, and Björn Wittrock, eds. *Axial Civilizations and World History.* Jerusalem Studies in Religion and Culture 4. Leiden: Brill, 2005.

Assmann, Jan. *God and the Gods: Egypt, Israel and the Rise of Monotheism.* Madison: University of Wisconsin Press, 2008.

Barnes, Michael H. *Stages of Thought: The Co-Evolution of Religious Thought and Science.* Oxford: Oxford University Press, 2000.

Bellah, Robert N. *Religion in Human Evolution: From the Paleolithic to the Axial Age.* Cambridge, Mass.: Harvard University Press, 2011.

———. "What Is Axial about the Axial Age?" *European Journal of Sociology* 46 (2005): 69–89.

Boardman, John. "Greek Art and Architecture." In Boardman, Griffin, and Murray, *Oxford History of the Classical World,* 275–309.

Boardman, John, Jasper Griffin, and Oswyn Murray, eds. *The Oxford History of the Classical World.* Oxford: Oxford University Press, 1986.

Bottéro, Jean. *Religion in Ancient Mesopotamia.* Translated by Teresa Lavender Fagan. Chicago: University of Chicago Press, 2001.

Boulding, Elise. "An Axial Age? Imagining Peace in the New Millennium." In *Principled World Politics: The Challenge of Normative International Relations,* edited by Paul Wapner and Lester E. J. Ruiz, 240–49. Lanham, Md.: Rowman & Littlefield, 2000.

Breuer, Stefan. "Kulturen der Achsenzeit: Leistung und Grenzen eines geschichtsphilosophischen Konzepts." *Saeculum* 45 (1994): 1–33.

Broughton, Jack M. "Pre-Columbian Human Impact on California Vertebrates: Evidence from Old Bones and Implications for Wilderness Policy." In Kay and Simmons, *Wilderness and Political Ecology,* 44–71.

Brown, Joseph Epes. *Teaching Spirits: Understanding Native American Religious Traditions.* With Emily Cousins. New York: Oxford University Press, 2001.

Burkert, Walter. *The Orientalizing Revolution: Near Eastern Influence on Greek Culture in the Early Archaic Age.* Translated by Margaret E. Pinder and Walter Burkert. Cambridge, Mass.: Harvard University Press, 1992.

Buss, Andreas. "The Evolution of Western Individualism." *Religion* 30 (2000): 1–25.

Cousins, Ewert H. *Christ of the 21st Century.* Rockport, Mass.: Element, 1992.

———. "Male-Female Aspects of the Trinity in Christian Mysticism." In *Sexual Archetypes, East and West*, edited by Bina Gupta, 37–50. New York: Paragon House, 1987.

———. "Spirituality in Today's World." In *Religion in Today's World: The Religious Situation of the World from 1945 to the Present Day*, edited by Frank Whaling, 306–34. Edinburgh: T&T Clark, 1987.

Crenshaw, James L. "Job, Book of." In *The Anchor Bible Dictionary*, edited by David Noel Freedman, 3:864–65. New York: Doubleday, 1996.

Diamond, Jared. *Guns, Germs and Steel: The Fates of Human Societies*. New York: Norton, 1997.

Donald, Merlin. *Origins of the Modern Mind: Three Stages in the Evolution of Culture and Cognition*. Cambridge, Mass.: Harvard University Press, 1991.

Edgar, Andrew. *Habermas: The Key Concepts*. London: Routledge, 2006.

Eisenstadt, Shmuel N. "The Axial Age Breakthroughs: Their Characteristics and Origins." In *The Origin and Diversity of Axial Age Civilizations*, edited by Shmuel N. Eisenstadt, 1–28. Albany: State University of New York, 1986.

———. "The Axial Age: The Emergence of Transcendental Visions and the Rise of Clerics." *European Journal of Sociology* 23 (1982): 294–314.

———. *Fundamentalism, Sectarianism, and Revolution: The Jacobin Dimension of Modernity*. Cambridge: Cambridge University Press, 1999.

Ellingson, Ter. *The Myth of the Noble Savage*. Berkeley: University of California Press, 2001.

Engelman, Robert. *More: Population, Nature and What Women Want*. Washington, D.C.: Island Press, 2008.

Fairchild, Hoxie Neale. *The Noble Savage: A Study in Romantic Naturalism*. New York: Columbia University Press, 1928.

Gillette, P. Roger. "A Religion for an Age of Science." *Zygon* 37 (2002): 461–71.

Griffin, Jasper. "Greek Myth and Hesiod." In Boardman, Griffin, and Murray, *Oxford History of the Classical World*, 78–98.

Guthrie, W. K. C. *A History of Greek Philosophy*. Vol. 1, *The Earlier Presocratics and the Pythagoreans*. Cambridge: Cambridge University Press, 1962.

Halpern, Baruch. *From Gods to God: The Dynamics of Iron Age*

Cosmologies. Edited by M. J. Adams. Forschungen zum Alten Testament 63. Tübingen: Mohr Siebeck, 2009.

Harbsmeier, Christoph. "The Axial Millennium in China." In Arnason, Eisenstadt, and Wittrock, *Axial Civilizations and World History*, 469–507.

Hazard, Paul. *The European Mind (1680–1715)*. London: Hollis & Carter, 1953.

Headland, Thomas. "Revisionism in Ecological Anthropology." *Current Anthropology* 38 (1997): 605–9.

Herbrechtsmeier, William E. "The Burden of the Axial Age: Transcendentalism in Religion as a Function of Empire." In *Defining Religion: Investigating the Boundaries between the Sacred and Secular*, edited by Arthur Greil and D. Bromley, 109–26. Religion and the Social Order 10. Amsterdam: JAI Press, 2003.

Hick, John. *An Interpretation of Religion: Human Responses to the Transcendent*. 2nd ed. New Haven, Conn.: Yale University Press, 2004.

Hobbes, Thomas. *Leviathan*, edited by Michael Oakeshott. Oxford: Basil Blackwell, 1946.

Holt, Flora Lu. "The Catch-22 of Conservation: Indigenous Peoples, Biologists and Cultural Change." *Human Ecology* 33 (2005): 199–215.

Hooykaas, Reijer. *Religion and the Rise of Modern Science*. Vancouver: Regent College, 2007.

Hsu Cho-Yun. "Rethinking the Axial Age: The Case of Chinese Culture." In Arnason, Eisenstadt, and Wittrock, *Axial Civilizations and World History*, 451–67.

Hughes, Glenn, Stephen A. McKnight, and Geoffrey L. Price, eds. *Politics, Order and History: Essays on the Work of Eric Voegelin*. Sheffield: Sheffield Academic, 2001.

Ingerson, Alice E. "Comments on Thomas Headland's 'Revisionism in Ecological Anthropology.'" *Current Anthropology* 38 (1997): 615–16.

"Interview with Nicanor González: We Are Not Conservationists; Indigenous Organizations Are Working at Every Level—Local, National, and International." *Cultural Survival Quarterly* 16, no. 3 (1992). http://www.culturalsurvival.org/publications/cultural-survival-quarterly/colombia/interview-nicanor-gonzalez-we-are-not-conservation, accessed February 8, 2012

Jaspers, Karl. "The Axial Age of Human History: A Base for the Unity of Mankind." *Commentary* 6 (1948): 430–35.

———. *The Origin and the Goal of History.* Translated by M. Bullock. New Haven, Conn.: Yale University Press, 1953.

———. *Vom Ursprung und Ziel der Geschichte.* Zurich: Artemis, 1949.

Jaspers, Karl, and Rudolf Bultmann. *Die Frage der Entmythologisierung.* Munich: Piper, 1954.

Jensen, Derrick. *Endgame.* Vol. 1, *The Problem of Civilization.* New York: Seven Stories, 2006.

Joas, Hans. "The Cultural Values of Europe: An Introduction." In *The Cultural Values of Europe*, edited by Hans Joas and Klaus Wiegandt, translated by Alex Skinner, 1–21. Liverpool: Liverpool University Press, 2008.

Kay, Charles E. "Afterword: False Gods, Ecological Myths, and Biological Reality." In Kay and Simmons, *Wilderness and Political Ecology*, 238–61.

———. "Are Ecosystems Structured from the Top-Down or Bottom-Up?" In Kay and Simmons, *Wilderness and Political Ecology*, 215–37.

Kay, Charles E., and Randy T. Simmons. *Wilderness and Political Ecology: Aboriginal Influences and the Original State of Nature.* Salt Lake City: University of Utah Press, 2002.

Kelly, Robert L. *The Foraging Spectrum: Diversity in Hunter-Gatherer Lifeways.* Washington, D.C.: Smithsonian Institution Press, 1995.

Kirch, Patrick V. "Oceanic Islands: Microcosms of 'Global Change.'" In Redman et al., *Archaeology of Global Change*, 13–27.

Knudtson, Peter, and David Suzuki. *Wisdom of the Elders.* Toronto: Stoddart, 1992.

Krech, Shepard, III. *The Ecological Indian: Myth and History.* New York: Norton, 1999.

Lambert, Yves. "Religion in Modernity as a New Axial Age: Secularization or New Religious Forms?" *Sociology of Religion* 60 (1999): 303–33.

Lawrence, Marc, Katie Ford, and Caryn Lucas. *Miss Congeniality.* Directed by Donald Petrie (Castle Rock Entertainment, 2000).

LeBlanc, Steven. *Constant Battles: The Myth of the Peaceful, Noble Savage.* New York: St. Martin's Press, 2003.

Levin, Harry. *The Myth of the Golden Age in the Renaissance.* Bloomington: Indiana University Press, 1969.

Levy, David J. "The Religion of Light: On Mani and Manichaeism." In Arnason, Eisenstadt, and Wittrock, *Axial Civilizations and World History*, 319–36.

Liverani, Mario. *Israel's History and the History of Israel.* Translated by Chiara Peri and Philip R. Davies. London: Equinox, 2005.

Lovejoy, Arthur O. "The Supposed Primitivism of Rousseau's Discourse on Inequality." *Modern Philology* 21 (1923): 165–86.

Low, Bobbi S. "Behavioral Ecology of Conservation in Traditional Societies." *Human Nature* 7 (1996): 353–79.

Ludwig, Theodore M. *The Sacred Paths: Understanding the Religions of the World.* 4th ed. Upper Saddle River, N.J.: Pearson Prentice Hall, 2006.

MacCulloch, Diarmaid. "The Axis of Goodness." *Guardian*, March 17, 2006. http://www.guardian.co.uk/books/2006/mar/18/higher education.news.

MacIntyre, Alasdair. *After Virtue: A Study in Moral Theory.* Notre Dame, Ind.: University of Notre Dame Press, 1981.

Mahmoudi, Hoda. "The Permanence of Change: Contemporary Sociological and Baha'i Perspectives on Modernity." *The Journal of Baha'i Studies* 18 (2008): 41–76.

Martin, Paul S. "Prehistoric Extinctions: In the Shadow of Man." In Kay and Simmons, *Wilderness and Political Ecology*, 1–27.

Martin, Paul S., and Christine R. Szuter. "Revising the 'Wild West': Big Game Meets the Ultimate Keystone Species." In Redman et al., *Archaeology of Global Change*, 63–88.

Mayer, John D. "Why Did People Change in the Axial Age?" The Personality Analyst. *Psychology Today.* June 15, 2009. http://www.psychologytoday.com/blog/the-personality-analyst/200906/why-did-people-change-in-the-axial-age.

Michalowski, Piotr. "Mesopotamian Vistas on Axial Transformations." In Arnason, Eisenstadt, and Wittrock, *Axial Civilizations and World History*, 157–81.

Momigliano, Arnaldo. *Alien Wisdom: The Limits of Hellenization.* Cambridge: Cambridge University Press, 1975.

Montmarquet, James A. "Jaspers, the Axial Age, and Christianity." *American Catholic Philosophical Quarterly* 83 (2009): 239–54.

Morgan, Lewis Henry. *Ancient Society: Researches in the Lines of Human Progress from Savagery Through Barbarism to Civilization.* New York: Henry Holt, 1877.

Morrow, William. "The Affirmation of Divine Righteousness in Early Penitential Prayers: A Sign of Judaism's Entry into the Axial Age." In *The Origins of Penitential Prayer in Second Temple Judaism*, edited by Mark J. Boda, Daniel K. Falk, and Rodney A. Werline, 101–17. Vol. 1 of *Seeking the Favor of God*. Atlanta: Society of Biblical Literature, 2006.

Muesse, Mark. *The Hindu Traditions: A Concise Introduction*. Minneapolis, Minn.: Fortress, 2011.

Neumann, Thomas W. "The Role of Prehistoric Peoples in Shaping Ecosystems in the Eastern United States: Implications for Restoration Ecology and Wilderness Management." In Kay and Simmons, *Wilderness and Political Ecology*, 141–78.

Obeyesekere, Gananath. *Imagining Karma: Ethical Transformation in Amerindian, Buddhist, and Greek Rebirth*. Berkeley: University of California Press, 2002.

Parker, Robert. "Greek Religion." In Boardman, Griffin, and Murray, *Oxford History of the Classical World*, 254–74.

Pinker, Steven. *The Better Angels of Our Nature: Why Violence Has Declined*. New York: Penguin, 2011.

Pitts, Leonard, Jr. "When Lies Triumph over Facts, We're Done." *Miami Herald*, June 30, 2012. http://www.miamiherald.com/2012/06/30/2876574/when-lies-triumph-over-facts-were.html, accessed on September 7, 2012.

Pollock, Sheldon. "Axialism and Empire." In Arnason, Eisenstadt, and Wittrock, *Axial Civilizations and World History*, 397–450.

Prabhu, R. K., and U. R. Rao, eds. *The Mind of Mahatma Gandhi*. Ahmedabad, India: Navajivan Trust, 1960. http://www.mkgandhi.org/momgandhi/chap33.htm.

Provan, Iain. *Seriously Dangerous Religion: What the Old Testament Really Says and Why It Matters*. Waco, Tex.: Baylor University Press, forthcoming.

Quinn, Daniel. *Ishmael: A Novel*. New York: Bantam, 1992.

Redman, Charles L., Steven R. James, Paul Fish, and J. Daniel Rogers, eds. *The Archaeology of Global Change: The Impact of Humans on Their Environment*. Washington, D.C.: Smithsonian Books, 2004.

Roemischer, Jessica. "A New Axial Age: Karen Armstrong on the History—and the Future—of God." *EnlightenNext*. http://www.enlightennext.org/magazine/j31/armstrong.asp, accessed on May 20, 2011.

Schwartz, Benjamin I. "The Age of Transcendence." *Daedalus* 104, no. 2 (1975): 1–7.

Shaked, Shaul. "Zoroastrian Origins: Indian and Iranian Connections." In Arnason, Eisenstadt, and Wittrock, *Axial Civilizations and World History*, 183–200.

Shulman, David. "Axial Grammar." In Arnason, Eisenstadt, and Wittrock, *Axial Civilizations and World History*, 369–95.

Smith, Steven G. *Appeal and Attitude: Prospects for Ultimate Meaning*. Bloomington: Indiana University Press, 2005.

Snell, Daniel C. *Religions of the Ancient Near East*. Cambridge: Cambridge University Press, 2011.

Stark, Rodney. *Discovering God: The Origins of the Great Religions and the Evolution of Belief*. New York: HarperOne, 2007.

Stearman, Allyn MacLean. "Only Slaves Climb Trees: Revisiting the Myth of the Ecologically Noble Savage in Amazonia." *Human Nature* 5 (1994): 339–57.

Stephens, David W., and John R. Krebs. *Foraging Theory*. Monographs in Behavior and Ecology. Princeton, N.J.: Princeton University Press, 1986.

Stokes, Evelyn. "Māori, Pākehā, and a Tenurial Revolution." In *Environmental Histories of New Zealand*, edited by Eric Pawson and Tom Brooking, 35–51. Melbourne: Oxford University Press, 2002.

Suzuki, David. *The Legacy: An Elder's Vision for Our Sustainable Future*. Vancouver: Greystone Books, 2010.

———. *The Sacred Balance: Rediscovering Our Place in Nature*. Vancouver: Greystone Books, 1997.

Taylor, Bron. *Dark Green Religion: Nature Spirituality and the Planetary Future*. Berkeley: University of California Press, 2010.

Teasdale, Wayne. "Concluding Reflections: Toward a Second Axial Age." In *Embracing Earth: Catholic Approaches to Ecology*, edited by Albert J. LaChance and John E. Carroll, 255–75. Maryknoll, N.Y.: Orbis, 1994.

Tucker, Carlton H. "From the Axial Age to the New Age: Religion as a Dynamic of World History." *History Teacher* 27 (1994): 449–64.

Van Ness, John H. *The Internet and the New Transformation of Consciousness*. October, 2002, http://www.vngroup.com/Aoir/John.htm, accessed on May 5, 2011.

Voegelin, Eric. *Order and History*. 5 vols. Baton Rouge: Louisiana State University Press, 1956–1987.

———. *Plato*. Baton Rouge: Louisiana State University Press, 1957.

Wagner, Peter. "Palomar's Questions: The Axial Age Hypothesis, European Modernity and Historical Contingency." In Arnason, Eisenstadt, and Wittrock, *Axial Civilizations and World History*, 87–106.

Walton, John. *Ancient Near Eastern Thought and the Old Testament: Introducing the Conceptual World of the Hebrew Bible*. Grand Rapids: Baker Academic, 2006.

Wenke, Robert J. *Patterns in Prehistory: Humankind's First Three Million Years*. 4th ed. New York: Oxford University Press, 1999.

White, Lynn. "The Historical Roots of Our Ecologic Crisis." *Science* 155 (1967): 1203–7.

———. "The Historical Roots of Our Ecologic Crisis." In *Western Man and Environmental Ethics*, ed. I. G. Barbour, 18–30. Reading, Mass.: Addison-Wesley, 1973.

Williams, Gerald. "Aboriginal Use of Fire: Are There Any 'Natural' Plant Communities?" In Kay and Simmons, *Wilderness and Political Ecology*, 179–214.

Williams, Michael. *Americans and Their Forests: A Historical Geography*. Cambridge: Cambridge University Press, 1989.

Wilson, John. "Roots of Faith," Review of *The Great Transformation*, by Karen Armstrong. *New York Times*, April 30, 2006. http://www.nytimes.com/2006/04/30/books/review/30wilson.html, accessed on May 13, 2011.

Wordsworth, William. *Selected Poetry*, edited by Mark Van Doren. New York: Modern Library, 1950.

Zerzan, John. *Twilight of the Machines*. Port Townsend, Wash.: Feral House, 2008.

Author Index

Alvard, Michael, 69, 71–72, 74n15
Anderson, Atholl, 73n12, 74
Armstrong, Karen, 3–4, 14–18, 29,
    34–38, 43, 58, 83, 87–88, 107, 109–11
Arnason, Johann, 7n1, 19–24, 27, 28n32
Assmann, Jan, 31–33

Barnes, Michael, 13, 27–28
Bellah, Robert, 17, 20n5, 29, 31–34, 97n4
Boardman, John, 104n22–23, 105n25
Bottéro, Jean, 98n5
Boulding, Elise, 13
Bradley, Marion Zimmer, 45
Breuer, Stefan, 27
Broughton, Jack, 75n17, 75n21
Brown, Joseph, 71n5
Bultmann, Rudolph, 86n4
Burkert, Walter, 104n23
Buss, Andreas, 13n19

Cousins, Ewert, 7, 11–12, 13n22, 86–88
Crenshaw, James, 35

Diamond, Jared, 65n24, 75n17
Donald, Merlin, 31–34
Dryden, John, 61–62

Edgar, Andrew, 14n29
Edgerton, Robert, 66
Eisenstadt, Shmuel, 21–24, 31
Ellingson, Ter, 44n10, 61n10–61n11,
    62n12, 82n40, 85n2, 88, 89n11,
    93n22
Emerson, Ralph Waldo, 45
Engelman, Robert, 17

Fairchild, Hoxie Neale, 44n10

Gillette, Roger, 13, 30n4
Goldhill, Simon, 36, 58
González, Nicanor, 71
Griffin, Jasper, 104n23
Guthrie, W. K. C., 118n15

Habermas, Jürgen, 14n29
Halpern, Baruch, 17
Harbsmeier, Christoph, 31n6
Hazard, Paul, 61
Headland, Thomas, 62n14, 66, 82,
    84n1, 94n23
Herbrechtsmeier, William, 13
Hick, John, 3, 13–14, 29–31
Hobbes, Thomas, 61

Holt, Flora Lu, 80n35, 123–24
Hooykaas, Reijer, 105n24
Hughes, Glenn, 21n9

Ingerson, Alice, 84, 123, 126

Jaspers, Karl, 2–3, 7–18, 17n40, 19–28,
    26n27, 29, 31n8, 34, 34n21, 37–39,
    43, 47, 85–88, 96, 105
Jensen, Derrick, 1, 4, 41, 46, 48, 51–56,
    80, 89–91, 94, 115–19
Joas, Hans, 17

Kay, Charles, 75n16–17, 75n19, 79, 95,
    121–22, 125
Kelly, Robert, 57, 59n3, 59n5, 60n6–7,
    62–63, 67–68, 82n39
Kirch, Patrick, 66n27, 74n14
Knudtson, Peter, 50–51, 91n17, 92n18–
    19, 93n20
Krebs, John, 72n7

Lambert, Yves, 13
LeBlanc, Steven, 57, 63–66, 83, 94
Lescarbot, Marc, 62
Levin, Harry, 61n9
Levy, David, 118n17
Liverani, Mario, 14
Lovelock, James, 45
Lovejoy, Arthur, 44n10
Low, Bobbi, 5, 71n5, 79–80, 121–22
Ludwig, Theodore, 28n32, 118n14,
    119n18

MacCulloch, Diarmaid, 29, 38
MacIntyre, Alasdair, 122
Mahmoudi, Hoda, 17
Martin, Paul, 65, 65n22, 75, 75n17–18,
    75n20
Mayer, John, 17n35
McKnight, Stephen, 21n9
Melekian, Brad, 46
Michalowski, Piotr, 33n16
Momigliano, Arnaldo, 10n8
Montmarquet, James, 29, 34n21
Morgan, Lewis Henry, 59
Morrow, William, 14
Muesse, Mark, 17

Muir, John, 45

Neumann, Thomas, 69, 79

Obeyesekere, Gananath, 13, 28

Parker, Robert, 105
Pinker, Steven, 66n30
Pitts, Leonard, 127n14
Pollock, Sheldon, 31
Prabhu, R. K., 95
Price, Geoffrey, 21n9
Provan, Iain, 119n19

Quinn, Daniel, 45–46

Rao, U. R., 95
Roemischer, Jessica, 88n10

Schwartz, Benjamin, 10n8
Shaked, Shaul, 28n32
Shulman, David, 31n8
Smith, Steven, 14
Snell, Daniel, 98n5
Snyder, Gary, 45
Stark, Rodney, 97n2, 98n5, 99n9,
    103n18
Stearman, Allyn MacLean, 70–71, 123
Stephens, David, 72n7
Stokes, Evelyn, 114–15
Suzuki, David, 4, 46–56, 91–94
Szuter, Christine, 65, 65n22, 75, 75n18,
    75n20

Taylor, Bron, 3, 41, 43n7, 44–48, 56
Teasdale, Wayne, 12–13
Terena, Marcos, 71
Thoreau, Henry David, 45
Toynbee, Arnold, 25
Tucker, Carlton, 13

Van Ness, John, 13n22
Voegelin, Eric, 19, 21, 21n9, 24–27, 30,
    30n1, 86, 86n4–5, 118n16

Wagner, Peter, 34
Walton, John, 98n5–7, 99n8–11, 100n12,
    101n13–14, 102n15–17, 113n8

Watson, Paul, 46, 56
Wenke, Robert, 58n1-2, 81n38, 97n1, 97n3
White, Lynn, 111–14, 115
Williams, Gerald, 77–79, 124–25

Williams, Michael, 78n29
Wilson, John, 38
Wordsworth, William, 81

Zerzan, John, 41–44, 46–47, 55

Subject Index

Achsenzeit, 10n8, 14, 27n29
agriculture, 15, 42, 46–47, 54, 56–57, 60, 62, 77, 78n29
Ainu, 67
Akhenaten, 28, 32–33, 104n19
anthropocentrism, 45–46, 56
Archimedes, 8, 105
Aristotle, 34, 50
axial age, 1–6, 7–18, 8n2, 10n8, 12n14, 13n19, 13n22, 14n29–30, 17n39–40, 19–28, 20n5, 29–39, 30n4, 31n8, 32n16, 34n21, 41–43, 47–48, 51, 54–56, 81, 85–88, 94, 95–96, 105–6, 107, 109–11, 121–22, 126

Bronze Age, 98, 103–4
Buddha, 8, 105
Buddhism, 20, 23, 28, 31n6, 41, 54, 108,
buffalo, 65, 75–77, 80

Calusa, 67
Cherokee, 80
Chief Seattle, 92–94
China, 8–9, 14, 14n29, 19, 20, 20n5, 22–23, 25–27, 31, 31n6, 33, 34n21, 104–5
Christianity, 14n30, 23, 25–6, 28, 29–31, 31n6, 31n10, 34n21, 41, 50, 54–55, 91, 111,
civilization, 1, 4, 13, 13n19, 15, 17, 20n5, 21–24, 21n9, 35, 37, 42–43, 46–47, 51–55, 57, 59, 61–62, 65, 80–81, 89–91, 90n13, 96, 98, 104–5, 109, 116

Cocamilla, 70
comparative method, 58–63
complex societies, 57, 65, 97–105
Confucianism, 14n27, 41, 54, 108
Confucius, 8, 105, 109
"Crime in Prehistory" (symposium), 66

Daosim, 8, 19
dark green religion, 3, 41, 44–48, 44n10, 76, 81, 92, 111, 115, 123
Diamante Piro, 71–72
Dolní Veštonice, 64

ecological wisdom (aboriginal), 66, 69, 70–82, 123–24
Eden, 35, 62, 113–14, 124–25
egalitarianism, 60, 67–68
Egypt, 13, 22, 26, 28, 30–32, 35, 64, 97–105, 99n10, 104n19, 110
equality, 44n10, 46, 53, 62n12, 66–68, 69, 80, 90
evolution, 13, 13n19, 17, 26, 31–33, 32n11, 37, 48, 59
extinctions, 70–79, 75n17, 77n22

faith (biblical), 5, 8–12, 12n14, 14n30, 33, 35–38, 54–55, 86, 96, 107–119
fire, 48–49, 58, 73, 77–78, 78n29, 124–25
foraging theory, 46, 62–63, 67, 71–74, 72n7, 82

Gaia, 44–45

Gorotire Kayapó, 70–71, 123
Greece, 8, 13, 14n29, 19–21, 25, 31, 33–34, 54, 103–5

Harappan, 104
Hawaiian Islands, 74
Hebrew prophets, 8, 25, 30, 30n5, 36, 86, 105, 109, 111
Heraclitus, 8, 105
Hesiod, 104, 104n23
Hinduism, 17, 23, 50, 91, 118
Holocene, 43, 73
Homer, 8, 104–5
Huaorani, 123–24

India, 8–9, 13, 14n29, 19–20, 25, 27–28, 28n32, 31, 31n8, 33, 34n21, 105–6
Inuit, 63
Islam, 14n30, 23, 26, 28, 30–31, 31n10, 41, 50, 54, 91

Jeremiah, 107, 109–11
Job, 35, 37–38, 111
Ju/'hoansi (!Kung), 67–68
Judaism, 14n29–30, 23, 25–26, 30–31, 30n5, 41, 54, 91

Kuna, 71, 71n4
!Kung (Ju/'hoansi), 63

Lahontan, 61, 93
Laozi, 8, 105
Lascaux, 64
Lewis and Clark, 65, 75

"Man the Hunter" (conference), 60
Mangaia, 74
Māori, 72–74, 114–15
Mesolithic, 64
Mesopotamia, 22, 33n16, 35, 98–100, 102, 105, 113
Montagnai, 80
mundane, 21–23, 31–33

nature, 4, 12n14, 13, 17, 41–56, 46n21, 57, 61–62, 65, 69–82, 84, 90–92, 111–13, 123–27
Neolithic, 15, 36, 42–43, 58, 96–97

noble savage, 5, 44n10, 1, 61–63, 66, 69, 85n2, 123–24

Ofnet, 64
Old Testament, 5, 86, 108, 113–14, 116, 119

Paleolithic, 4, 14, 17, 36, 43, 56, 57–68, 69, 82, 96–97, 122
Parmenides, 8, 34, 105
passenger pigeon, 78–79
peace, 1–3, 6, 26n27, 45, 48, 53, 60, 63–66, 67, 69, 80, 82, 83, 88–90, 99
Plains Indians, 45, 75–80, 75n17, 77n22, 78n29
Plato, 8, 34, 50, 99n9, 105, 118
Pleistocene, 43, 75, 75n17

Rapa Nui (Easter Island), 74
religion, 1–3, 7–18, 11n14, 13n22, 14n27, 24–28, 29–34, 30n4, 31n10, 38, 41–47, 44n10, 49–51, 50n33, 54–55, 59, 69, 76, 80–82, 86–88, 90–92, 95–106, 107–119, 121, 123; aboriginal, 43, 49–51, 53, 80, 96–97; ancient Near Eastern, 32–33, 97–103; Greek, 31, 33–34, 103–5
Romanticism, 61–62, 81–82, 123
Rome, 13, 20, 92, 105, 118
Rousseau, 44, 44n10, 62n12, 82

Shang, 104
Siona-Secoya, 80n35
Socrates, 34
Stone Age, 13, 43, 52

Thucydides, 8, 105
transcendental, 21–24, 27, 31–34, 55–56
Tukanoan, 70

Upanishads, 8, 14n27, 20, 31, 105

violence, 5, 12–13, 15–16, 46, 51–56, 63–68, 65n24, 87–91, 90n13, 95, 105–6, 107–19, 121

wilderness, 6, 75n17, 78, 95, 102, 110, 121–22, 124–25

Yanomama, 65
Yellowstone National Park, 121, 125, 125n11
Yuquí, 70–71, 123

Zoroaster (Zarathustra), 8, 28, 28n32 105
Zoroastrianism, 28, 31